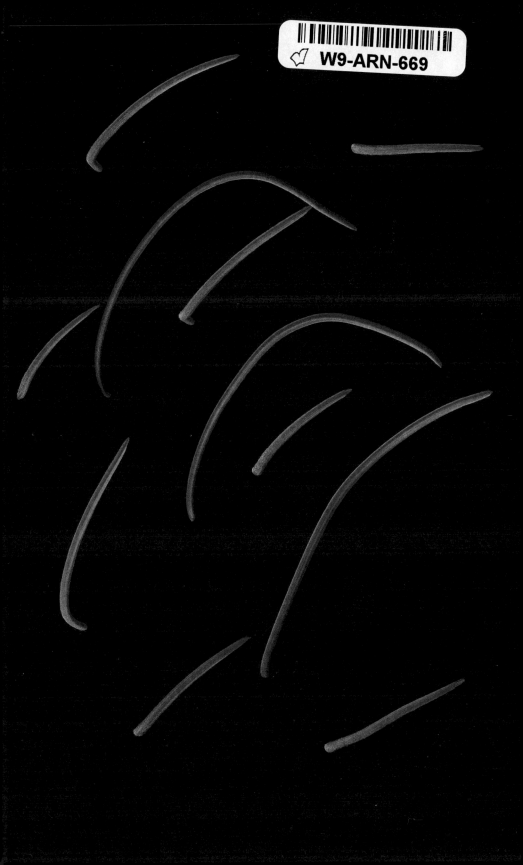

W9-ARN-669

PRAISE FOR *MANLY MEN*

"Stephen Mansfield gives us yet another fantastic book, this time covering a topic so misunderstood and misrepresented in society today. He creates a blueprint for true manhood, building upon stories from the world's greatest men—one of whom was my great-grandfather, Winston Churchill. I applaud Stephen for the massive research he has done. I will read this book again and again and learn something new every time. Mansfield truly is a 'Manly Man.'"

—JONATHAN SANDYS
great-grandson of Sir Winston Churchill

"I'm sick to death of seeing men portrayed as bumbling morons in movies and TV commercials. We're living in a culture that tries to make masculinity a punch line, and it's having a devastating effect on our families and society. In *Mansfield's Book of Manly Men*, Stephen takes the bold, potentially offensive step of calling men to be men again. It's about time!"

—DAVE RAMSEY
New York Times best-selling author and
nationally syndicated radio show host

"We live in such a fast-paced society and yet many of our men sit around and do nothing! It's time to get off the bench and get in the game. In *Mansfield's Book of Manly Men*, Stephen challenges us to do the very thing God has intended for us to do . . . act! To act like men and do what men do. Buckle your chinstrap before you pick up this book because it is truth and its challenge will hit you as you've never been hit. A must read for every man!"

—MARK BRUNELL
former NFL quarterback;
Head of Football, Episcopal School of Jacksonville

"*Mansfield's Book of Manly Men* cuts to the heart of what it means to be a true man. In a culture where authentic masculinity is often buried beneath myriad counterfeits and stereotypes, Mansfield's vision of manhood is a refreshing and challenging ideal. Replete with inspiring biographies of heroic men, interwoven with spiritual insight, this is a book of action, initiation, and honor. Society says being a real man means driving expensive cars, owning a big house, dominating a woman, and not being bound to anything except the advancement of your own career. In contrast, Mansfield reminds us that to be a true man is to be honest, humble, compassionate, responsible, courageous, and faithful. I hope many people read this book, including my sons."

—JONATHAN JACKSON
star of the hit ABC show *Nashville*

MANSFIELD'S BOOK
OF MANLY MEN

ALSO BY STEPHEN MANSFIELD

Never Give In:
The Extraordinary Character of Winston Churchill

Then Darkness Fled:
The Liberating Wisdom of Booker T. Washington

Forgotten Founding Father:
The Heroic Legacy of George Whitefield

The Faith of George W. Bush

The Faith of the American Soldier

Benedict XVI: His Life and Mission

The Faith of Barack Obama

The Search for God and Guinness

Lincoln's Battle with God

Killing Jesus

MANSFIELD'S BOOK OF MANLY MEN

An Utterly Invigorating Guide to Being
Your Most Masculine Self

STEPHEN MANSFIELD

NELSON
BOOKS

Published in Nashville, Tennessee, by Nelson Books, an imprint of Thomas Nelson. Nelson Books and Thomas Nelson are registered trademarks of HarperCollins Christian Publishing, Inc.

Thomas Nelson, Inc., titles may be purchased in bulk for educational, business, fund-raising, or sales promotional use. For information, please e-mail SpecialMarkets@ThomasNelson.com.

Scripture quotations marked ESV are from the ENGLISH STANDARD VERSION. © 2001 by Crossway Bibles, a division of Good News Publishers.

Scripture quotations marked NET are from the New English Translation, NET Bible.® Copyright © 1996–2006 by Biblical Studies Press, L.L.C. http://netbible.com. All rights reserved.

Scripture quotations marked NIV are from the Holy Bible, New International Version®, NIV®. © 1973, 1978, 1984, 2011 by Biblica, Inc.™ Used by permission of Zondervan. All rights reserved worldwide. www.zondervan.com.

Poems without citations are in the public domain.

Original illustrations by Clint Hansen.

Interior page design by Walter Petrie.

Library of Congress Cataloging-in-Publication Data

Mansfield, Stephen, 1958–
  Mansfield's book of manly men : an utterly invigorating guide to being your most masculine self / Stephen Mansfield.
     pages cm
  Includes bibliographical references.
  ISBN 978-1-59555-373-7
  1. Men—Conduct of life. 2. Men Christian theology) I. Title.
  BJ1601.M36 2013
  248.8'42—dc23   2013016866

Printed in the United States of America

14 15 16 17 RRD 6

To Jim Laffoon

Pride of the 82nd Airborne Division
Pride of the millions he has taught
Pride of the author, his friend

CONTENTS

CONTENTS

FOREWORD

by
Lieutenant General William G. Boykin (retired)
Former commander, Delta Force

FEW PERSONALITIES IN THE BIBLE ARE MORE RECOGNIZED FOR their manly qualities than the "man after God's own heart," the great King David. He was an extraordinary warrior, an accomplished musician, a skilled author, a man of great wisdom, and, as important, a dutiful shepherd over his father's flocks. He was also courageous, passionate, and certainly flawed. David was a manly man who achieved greatness in his lifetime, a man all men today should study for the lessons they can learn.

David knew what it was to be a man. As he lay dying, he called his son Solomon to his bedside and gave him final instructions: "I am about to go the way of all the earth. So be strong and show yourself a man." These are the last recorded words of one of the greatest kings to ever live. Of all he might have said to his son with his final breath, he chose to instruct him to be a man. They are words we should never forget.

Today the concept of being a manly man is something every American male should contemplate. The truth is most men are not at all clear about what it means to be a real man in American society. The feminist movement has severely reworked the image of manhood, and this has damaged the self-esteem of many men. Likewise, the constant intrusion of government into the family structure in our nation has contributed dramatically to confusion about what God intends men to be. When a government perpetuates the myth that its programs are more important than fathers in the home, men will naturally suffer a crisis of identity.

Men also face the popular but false notion that women can do anything a man can do. This, too, serves to emasculate men, just as it ignores God's highest and noblest intentions for men and women. It has given our nation a plague of gender confusion that masquerades as trendy gender neutrality and leaves us everything from unisex dress to mixing the sexes in frontline combat units in our military. This is one of many signs of America's deepening gender crisis, a crisis that is devastating American men.

Sadly, most Christian churches offer little help in this cause, and it is because they fail to articulate the true nature of the greatest man in history, Jesus Christ. Many churches portray him as meek, weak, and almost effeminate. This leads to men who are much the same.

It is a picture far from the true Jesus Christ. Consider for a moment. Jesus was a carpenter who worked with his hands and lifted heavy stone and large chunks of wood. His hands were calloused and scarred from the everyday wear and tear of carpentry. Yes, he was the Son of God, but he was also a man's man. He even told his disciples to sell their cloaks and buy swords as they set off to do his work and build his church. He was establishing for their understanding that there are things worth fighting for, even things worth dying for as men.

He is our highest example of manhood, particularly in the magnificence of his courage. We should never forget how he entered the temple in Jerusalem one day. Seeing conduct that showed disregard for the honor of God, he made a braided whip and drove moneychangers and merchants out of the temple courts. You can bet that those who saw him do it never forgot how he flipped over tables and fiercely prevented strong young men from carrying merchandise through God's house. This is the true Jesus Christ. He was tough and rugged, but also the epitome of love and compassion.

What about American men today?

Most modern men do not reflect the image of the best model for genuine manhood. Society suffers as a result. For example, many men are convinced it is somehow manly to produce children yet unmanly to take responsibility for them. This is why there are American households teeming with children but absent a father.

Consider also the domestic abuse statistics in America. What kind of degenerate thinks it is manly to beat a woman—that he is somehow affirming his superior status in the world through violence against those he is intended to protect?

I could ask the same question about men who have extramarital affairs. What kind of man breaks his vows, destroys lives, and violates the laws of God for false love and brief pleasures?

It must be the same kind of man who allows pornography—a kind of fictional intimacy of the imagination—to destroy genuine intimacy with a loving wife. Certainly men who do these things are not modeling themselves after the ultimate man, Jesus Christ.

It is no wonder so many people are asking these days, "Where are all the real men?"

Manhood is suffering today. Men seem to be confused about what God wants them to be and about how to live out their manly calling. I often get this question from the men I meet: "Are there any examples of real men that we can emulate?" I answer, "Yes!" Let me tell you about just one.

My dad was a manly man who was a fine role model for my brother and me. Gerald Boykin grew up on a tobacco farm in eastern North Carolina as one of ten children. He was the sixth son of a sharecropper. Gerald dropped out of high school three months after his seventeenth birthday so he could join the United States Navy during World War

II. His four older brothers were already deployed to combat zones and Gerald refused to stay behind. He simply had to join his brothers in upholding what they all believed.

Knowing my father as I do, I'm sure he also did not want to be left out of the war stories that would be told at the family gatherings in later years!

His passion to serve his country like a man landed him in the middle of fierce fighting on June 6, 1944—D-Day. Gerald was severely wounded and left blind in his left eye. After his discharge from the navy, he returned to the tobacco farm, married his sweetheart, and started a family. When the Korean War began in 1950, he returned to service in the United States Army, which had a program for disabled veterans who could still function. After the war, he was discharged a second time. Upon leaving the army, Gerald accepted a job with the United States Marine Corps, where he served for thirty-two years as a federal employee. This service included a year in Vietnam and multiple deployments into dangerous areas.

Gerald never expected America to give him anything but an opportunity. He served his nation with devotion all his life and raised his family to love God and to love the nation that he had so faithfully served. His sense of justice and his moral courage were his cornerstone characteristics. Gerald knew what he believed, what was important to him, and what he was unwilling to compromise. He had a servant's heart and the strength of character to stand by his convictions. He had transcendent causes in his life. They can be summarized in three words: God, country, family.

Though he had little education, Gerald was a man of wisdom who took his responsibilities as a father and mentor seriously and always stood on principle. His sense of right and wrong gave him the moral compass that guided his life. He never blamed others for his own failures or shortcomings. He accepted responsibility for his actions and lived with the consequences. He was my hero—a real man, a manly man.

Some readers probably expected me to characterize him as a skilled hunter or fisherman or outdoorsman or even an avid golfer. After all, isn't that what we think of when we talk about manly men these days? Well, he was all of these things, too, but they were not what made him a manly man. Instead, it was his willingness to subordinate his own desires and aspirations to greater causes: his God, his nation, and his family. He put the welfare and security of others before his own. He knew he was blessed by a sovereign and loving God to be an American, and he believed his family was a gift from God for which he was responsible.

Some readers might also have expected me to brag about my father's physical strength. Yeah, he was a powerful man, too, with enough strength to impress other men. Yet this did not make him manly either. Physical strength is never what makes a man manly. Rather, it is moral strength that identifies the true man, and my father had plenty of it. He was the kind of man King David called his son to be.

What about you? Are you a manly man? Can you call yourself a real warrior, a protector of the flock, a man with a transcendent cause in your life?

Sadly, too many men in America cannot identify with the characteristics of a real man. The ideal of the warrior, for example, is too high for them. What makes a man a warrior is his willingness to place himself between what he holds dear and anything that threatens it. Honor is the chief motivator for the warrior. Dishonor is unthinkable. He does the right thing without expectation of reward because honor is an intrinsic value that, when manifested in one's life, provides its own rewards.

The protector of the flock will risk his own life just as King David did when his father's sheep were threatened by a lion and a bear. Although

David certainly feared the strength and aggression of the bear and the lion, he overcame that fear because he knew the power of his God was greater. We should remember this. A manly man is not without fear; rather he overcomes his fear by enduring difficulty and hardship. Also, like King David, he knows the source of his own strength: God himself.

Each man must determine what is dear to him and what is worth sacrificing for. A transcendent cause must exist in a man's life if he is to reach his full potential as a man. Few men today have done a thorough self-analysis to ascertain what their transcendent cause is—or even if they have one. It is time, though: time to determine what we hold dear and what is worthy of sacrifice. As men, we cannot wait until the later years of our lives to make this assessment. I urge you: do it now, and bring meaning to who you are as a man.

I was privileged to serve for thirty-six years in the United States Army with some of America's finest men. Because I was in Special Operations, I served with people who were selected because they were the best in their fields and were totally committed to their beliefs and values. I have seen them do extraordinary things, often at the risk of their lives.

During the Blackhawk Down events in Mogadishu, Somalia, in October of 1993, two of my Delta Force men, Randy Shughart and Gary Gordon, sacrificed their lives to save four comrades who had crashed in a helicopter in a hostile part of the city. Knowing there was no one else who could save their comrades at that moment, these two men volunteered to go alone into what they knew was almost certainly a fatal situation. After asking three times to be allowed to save the four men in the crash, they were finally granted permission to go.

Ultimately, only the copilot survived to tell the story of how these incredible heroes jumped from a hovering helicopter and fought their way into the crash where they removed the crew from their seats and then defended them until they were killed. These men were motivated by more than self-interest. They were patriots. They were men.

They, and many like them, are still the core of American manhood. I am actually optimistic today because there are other men like Shughart and Gordon who are not only serving in our nation's armed forces, but are serving in numerous ways in communities across the nation. Some are professionals, but many are factory workers, farmers, and average citizens who have settled the question of what they care most about and are prepared to make sacrifices for the things they value. These are the leaders of the future.

Stephen Mansfield has provided an extraordinary blueprint for every man to determine how he can be the man that God has called him to be—a manly man. Stephen uses his knowledge of biblical principles combined with his incredible understanding of men—and the influences and distractions that they are facing today—to show us how to grow into the kind of man that King David wanted Solomon to be.

This book is a must read for every American male. We must restore the understanding of what it means to be a manly man. The nation's future depends on men getting back to the fundamentals of being men of courage and values. Read this book and discover what it means to be a manly man. What you find may surprise you. You will be changed for the better and inspired to be the man you want to be—the man God intended you to be.

PART ONE

To do an evil action is base: to do a good action without incurring danger is common enough; but it is part of a good man to do great and noble deeds, though he risks everything.

Plutarch, reported in Dictionary of Burning Words of Brilliant Writers *by Josiah H. Gilbert (1895)*

Christian life is action: not a speculating, not a debating, but a *doing*. One thing, and only one, in this world has eternity stamped upon it. Feelings pass; resolves and thoughts pass; opinions change. What you have *done* lasts—lasts in you. Through the ages, through eternity, what you have done for Christ—that, and only that, you are.

Frederick W. Robertson (1816–1853), from Sermons Preached at Trinity Chapel, Brighton, v. III *(1859)*

Our grand business is not to see what lies dimly at a distance, but to do what lies clearly at hand.

Thomas Carlyle, from Carlyle's essay "Signs of the Times," which originally appeared in the Edinburgh Review *in 1829*

GENTLEMEN, WE BEGIN . . .

Let me start by telling you about the night I became a man.

Years ago, I was traveling through the Middle East to do relief work in a troubled country. A problem arose with my visa. If all had gone according to plan, I would have flown into Damascus, traveled nine hours through the Syrian Desert, crossed the Euphrates River, and entered Iraq. I had done it several times before. On this particular trip, I never got out of Damascus.

I know this sounds like the start of a great adventure. It wasn't. I spent my days at the Damascus Sheraton eating bad hamburgers and arguing about Syrian football with the doorman like I knew enough to have an opinion. Now don't misunderstand: I'm going to tell this to my grandchildren like I'm Lawrence of Arabia, but you should know it wasn't true. I was bored. I ate pistachio nuts by the pound. I read everything I could find that was printed in English. I even got fitted for a *bisht*—the elegant outer robe Arab men sometimes wear. I had it made, put it on once, decided I looked regal, and then never wore it again. These were not my most productive days.

Fortunately, a friend of mine who was a member of the Syrian parliament heard I was stranded and came to my rescue. We'll call him

Nadeem. He was a cool breeze of Arab hospitality. He took me to meet officials who could help me, feasted me at the finest restaurants in the city, and insisted that I go with him to his Orthodox church, though he knew I would not understand a word. When I reluctantly went with him that next Sunday morning, I found language no barrier. Hugs from little old Syrian ladies told me everything I needed to know. Nadeem knew they would. He was a good friend to me during those days.

It was because of Nadeem that I ended up on the roof of a hotel in downtown Damascus with a dozen Arab men. That's where I became a man.

Nadeem knew I was lonely, and he also wanted to show off his American friend, so he decided to host a small party. I urged him not to bother, but he insisted as though all honor depended upon it. Several nights later, I found myself atop a soaring Damascus hotel surrounded by high-ranking government officials, their submachine gun–toting bodyguards, several expensively dressed businessmen, and one man in a *shemagh*—the traditional Arab cloth headdress—who looked to me as though he had just come in from the desert. Of course, the desert was about three blocks away.

It was a stunningly clear Syrian night. The tents on that rooftop seemed to breathe with the evening breezes drifting in from the sand. It was mystical, and I wanted desperately to be still and quiet to take it all in.

Nadeem had other plans. He began by eagerly introducing me to his friends, and then he insisted I recount my life since birth along with everything he and I had ever discussed. This got the party started, meaning we spoke to each other as well as we could—which was badly—while we ate cashews the size of a man's thumb and bowls of watermelon. Some of the older ones smoked the *nargillah*, the intriguing Arab water pipe often called a *hookah*. All were gracious and interested, but there was only so much we could manage to communicate through our limited knowledge of each other's languages, and the conversation inevitably lagged.

That's when the more traditional-looking man wearing the *shemagh* leaned forward and asked a question. There was great wonder in his face, as though he was inquiring about one of the great mysteries of God.

It turned out he was.

"A son. Do you have?" he asked. I'm telling you every man on that roof stopped what he was doing and turned to hear my answer.

"I do," I replied.

"Ah." He grew excited. "His name?"

"Jonathan," I answered.

The man slapped his knee and shouted, "Aha! Then you have a new name! You are Abujon!" Suddenly, there was a lot of smiling and head nodding and Arab voices one on top of the other.

They could tell I didn't understand. Nadeem tried to explain. Apparently, when an Arab man has a son, his name changes. From that moment on, he is addressed with a combination of *Abu*, which means father, and the name of his son. Apparently, Arabs consider fatherhood so important that once a man becomes a father to a son, he is honored for it the rest of his life.

So I became Abujon.

When this was announced, that rooftop erupted. Men started shaking my hand and slapping me on the back. Food arrived by the platter-full: the best lamb I've ever had and *naan* and a dozen types of *baklava*. It just wouldn't end. After a while, music sounded from somewhere, and several of the men started teaching me an Arab dance, one holding his submachine gun in his other hand. It was a *night*! Finally, at three or four in the morning, they drove me back to the Sheraton and backslapped me out the car door.

"Gooood nyett, Abujon!"

I went to my room and, as spent as I was, I sat up hours longer staring out the window at the brilliant Damascus night. Something had happened to me. I could feel it but couldn't put words to it. I think I was afraid that if I didn't explain it to myself I would wake up the next morning and find that this powerful new thing was gone.

It came to me a day or two later. At first it was a great sadness, and then it became a ferocity and strength that has never left me.

I should tell you this: by the time of that night in Damascus, I was forty-one years old. I had been a Christian for twenty-three years. I had been a husband for seventeen years. I had been a father for thirteen years.

Yet never before in all of my life had I ever been welcomed into the fellowship of men. Not once. Not ever. Nor had I ever undergone any sort of ritual to mark any of the important turning points in my life as a man. No one had ever said to me, "Congratulations. You are now a man among men."

Frankly, I didn't know I needed to hear it.

When the moment finally did come, it was a gift of Arab men who issued the welcome with hardly a word. They named me. They celebrated me. They gave me gifts. They made it clear they understood. They counted me as one of their own.

It is impossible to fully describe what all this has meant since. The impact of that night is probably best captured in a single word: *honor*. Now, I had not lacked for honor in my life before that moment. I grew up the son of a decorated US Army officer. I eagerly played three sports a year in my youth and was recruited to play college football. I had friends who were sworn to me and I to them. I knew a bit about honor.

Still, never had I been honored in such a way that it summoned dormant forces from within me. Never before had honor given definition to my life, sealed me to men of common experience, or imparted meaning.

Yet all this and more had happened on that extraordinary night.

Stirring new perspectives embedded themselves in my mind. To be a man. To have a son. To suddenly understand manhood as both a life to live and a tribe to belong to. For all my years yet to come, to be shaped by the calm, fierce knowing that I would live them as a man—not merely as a male—and as a father. To know the good this could be for those I loved.

All of this was born of that night. Yet it has taken me more words to describe the experience here than were spoken during all the hours on that rooftop. Some of the most important things about my life were defined that evening without any of them having been described or explained. I suppose this is the power of ritual, commemoration, and tradition. They impart more than they explain, summon more than was thought available.

Perhaps there is a lesson for us in this. I will risk offending—and not for the last time in these pages, I'm sure—by saying I suspect if such a moment had taken place somewhere in the Western world, it would have come with a torrent of words. It would have been talked to death. It would have come with a book, a seminar, a CD series, hours of concerned discussion, two recommended websites, a retreat, and a certificate to put on the wall. We'd probably still be talking about it . . . having never actually done anything.

My friends in Syria lived differently. They arrived at the all-important word—*Abujon*—with two short questions. Once they ecstatically proclaimed it, they didn't have a great deal more to say. They didn't bother to explain much. In fact, they didn't even ask my permission. They just declared it and then celebrated my life in the tribe of men with the fiercest, manliest partying I've ever seen. Six hours later, they pushed me out the door.

"Go. Be a man. Be a father. Remember that you are part of us."

I had been a *male* for more than four decades when that night occurred. I learned in those hours, however, that you are not fully a *man* until you are a man among men who respect what it means to be a man—and who know how to summon manhood through honor.

My goal in this book is simple. I want to identify what a genuine man does—the virtues, the habits, the disciplines, the duties, the actions of true manhood—and then call men to do it. I mean exactly these words. This book is about doing. It is about action. There is certainly an appropriate moment for men to talk about their pasts, their wounds, theories of manhood, questions of values, and their ongoing war with the society around them. This isn't it. This book is about knowing the deeds that comprise manhood and doing those deeds until mere males become genuine men. For fun and for simplicity, I call these genuine men *manly men* in these pages.

My conviction—and it underlies all that is ahead—is that we become what we do, that we are the sum of our habits. I should say quickly I do not believe we are *only* the sum of our habits. I am a Christian, and so I believe there is more at work in our lives than the product of what we do. Thank God! To be a Christian is to believe the grace of Jesus breaks the unending, hellish cycle of cause and effect. I don't want to live forever in the cancerous wake of my evil deeds. Grace intervenes. The Spirit makes me new. I'm freed, even from myself.

Trust me, I get all this and have based my life upon it. Still, even after grace comes to us, virtues have to be perfected. Our habits have to be formed. Our actions have to be aligned with the grace we have received.

We often miss this emphasis in Scripture. Consider just one verse on the subject: "Make every effort to add to your faith goodness; and to goodness, knowledge; and to knowledge, self-control; and to self-control, perseverance; and to perseverance, godliness; and to godliness, mutual affection; and to mutual affection, love. For if you possess these qualities in increasing measure, they will keep you from being ineffective and unproductive in your knowledge of our Lord Jesus Christ" (2 Peter 1:5–8 NIV). Clearly, we are given faith and we are taught knowledge, but to make both productive, we have to devote ourselves to a lifelong project of developing traits, attitudes, and habits. The apostle Peter calls them qualities in these verses. Otherwise, we'll be "ineffective and unproductive" despite the grace and knowledge we possess.

If we lived in an ideal world, every man would learn the traits of manliness as part of a dynamic body of righteous men. He would have models in these older men. He would have a tribe. He would be initiated, honored, challenged, trained, corrected, and commissioned by these men. In fact, in an ideal world, a man would barely be able to identify what had made him a great man, a genuine man. It would all be natural and woven into life. It would just *be*.

Most of us have never had anything like this. Almost none of us. It is a loss, but it doesn't have to mean devastation. Instead, it means we have to put ourselves in a position to absorb the manly virtues another way. That's why I've written this book.

I intend here to put us among true men. I'm going to describe the characteristics of vital manhood as illustrated in some of the great lives of history, lives that reveal what we must do to be true men. These men are part of what the New Testament calls our "cloud of witnesses." I think of the men in these pages as our cloud of witnesses to manliness.

Imagine sitting with Winston Churchill and asking him what he had to overcome to be a great man. Imagine asking this same question of Booker T. Washington or Rudyard Kipling or Jonathan, son of King Saul. I think using inspiring tales from the lives of great men of the past makes the journey fascinating. I think it connects us with a heritage and points us toward a destiny. It also gives us tools for defining manhood for the next generation of men, those who look to us to show them what to do. We want to give them far more than we received. The great men of history—our fathers, in a broad sense—help us do this.

Fear not, though; this will not be some dusty volume of dates and dead people. History can be more than that. It lives. It breathes. It can be rowdy and fun. It has power and nobility to impart.

The great men of old have much to offer us, and we should not neglect their gifts. In these pages, we won't.

There are a few important matters to settle before we begin.

The first is the issue of women. It is an evil of our age—perhaps of every age—that there is tension and competition between the genders. Do a search for the word *men* on the Internet and most of what you find is about the antagonisms, animosities, and disappointments that separate men and women. Most of what is "for" men is inherently "against" women. The reverse is also true.

Let's be clear. This book is about men being strong, moral, dutiful, virtuous men—frankly, great men—in part because it is the best gift we can give to women. There is nothing in this book that diminishes women, dismisses women, or denigrates women. Instead, much of this book is about how a man is measured in large part by who he is for the women in his life. I can certainly understand why some women might fear a book about how men can be "true men." This has not always worked out well for women in the past. Trust me, women will only gain from what this book encourages in their men.

Having said this, though, I should also say that this book is *Cosc ar cailíní*, as our Irish-speaking friends would say: "Not for girls!"

Second, we live in an age that defines people largely by appearance. The body *is* the man. The look *is* the woman. There is almost no separating the outer from the inner, the true man from the physical vessel he occupies in this life.

This overemphasis on what is seen has had tragic consequences for some men. Some of us just don't look "manly" in the traditional sense. We are thin or un-muscular or high-voiced or perhaps even effeminate in the way we move. These features tempt us to believe that we are condemned to some form of un-manly, un-masculine life. Meanwhile, our more hairy, more muscular friends are considered manly merely for their appearance.

Hear me: I don't care about your appearance. Manliness, in my view, is about doing. It doesn't matter what you look like. I'm neither put off by nor in awe of the physical. I've known great men who are three and a half feet tall. I know an awe-inspiring man who has no arms or legs. I've known powerful, dynamic men who looked like women from a distance. I've known immoral men who had testosterone to spare. It is the doing, the deeds, the actions that make a male a man.

This is good news. Any man, no matter his appearance or voice, can be a great man, because masculine greatness is about the doing, not about the appearance. This means that the guy with the squeaky voice and the twenty-eight-inch waist and the walk that he wishes he could change can be a man in the truest sense. It also means that the guy with the twenty-eight-inch bicep is responsible for the same standard of manliness, no matter his physique. True manliness is about the determination to act according to a noble definition of what it means to be a man. This is within the reach of every man, no matter how he looks or sounds.

Finally, I must say this: it is time for unfathered men to stop waiting for someone to father them. I know this sounds harsh. I've had to be corrected by these words myself. If you've had a loving, devoted father or father figure in your life, wonderful! He is a gift. Some of us haven't had this kind of male mentoring, and so we can be tempted to sit around hoping that one day an older, wiser man will swoop down upon us and impart the secrets of life. It is not likely to happen. While we wait, we miss the opportunities before us and the role we could play in our world.

To illustrate this, I'll use a scene from that grand metaphor for the meaning of life, *The Andy Griffith Show*. Every great and eternal truth is portrayed somewhere in this classic series. In the episode I refer to, Andy Taylor, the sheriff of Mayberry, is out of town. His deputy, Barney Fife (famously played by Don Knotts) is in charge, and he has deputized the local mechanic whose name is Gomer (famously played by Jim Nabors).

The two deputies are walking down the street one evening when they notice that someone is robbing the bank. They hide behind a car. They are afraid and don't quite know what to do. Finally, Gomer looks at Barney and says excitedly, "Shazam! We need to call the police!"

In utter exasperation, Barney shoots back: "We *are* the police!"

This is very much like the predicament of many men today. They know something is wrong. They aren't whole, haven't been fathered, and are confused about what it means to be men. They have no idea what to do. They want to call someone. They're waiting for rescue. It doesn't come.

Then they look around and realize that no one is ever going to drop into their lives and teach them what they need to know. They are going to have to get it themselves. They *are* "the police." They may even have to band together and help each other make up lost ground in this business of being a man. In fact, as unsure as they are, others are looking to *them* to be fathers and looking to *them* to define what it means to be a man.

There's only one thing to do: man up. Learn quickly. Time is slipping by, and a generation is waiting.

I trust this book will make the job easier. Let's get to it.

—*Stephen Mansfield*

GIVE US MEN!

Give us Men!
Men—from every rank,
Fresh and free and frank;
Men of thought and reading,
Men of light and leading,
Men of loyal breeding,
The nation's welfare speeding;
Men of faith and not of fiction,
Men of lofty aim in action;
Give us Men—Oh, I say again,
Give us Men!

Give us Men!
Strong and stalwart ones;
Men whom highest hope inspires,
Men whom purest honor fires,
Men who trample self beneath them,
Men who make their country wreath them
As her noble sons,
Worthy of their sires;
Men who never shame their mothers,
Men who never fail their brothers,
True, however false are others:
Give us Men—I say again,
Give us Men!

Give us Men!
Men who, when the tempest gathers,

Grasp the standard of their fathers
In the thickest fight;
Men who strike for home and altar,
(Let the coward cringe and falter),
God defend the right!
True as truth the lorn and lonely,
Tender, as the brave are only,
Men who treat where saints have trod,
Men for Country, Home- and God:
Give us Men! I say again—again—
Give us Men!

—JOSIAH GILBERT HOLLAND

THE MANLY MAXIMS

MEN ARE IN CRISIS. WE KNOW THIS. THERE ARE BOOKS ABOUT it, seminars about it, retreats about it, academic conferences about it, and every kind of gathering where men sit around and talk about it. As these words are being written, men lag behind women in nearly every measurable field of achievement. If the statistics are true, and if television commercials are any reflection, men today are unhappy, self-loathing, pleasure-addicted, juvenile, and less productive than ever.

Three recent book titles tell the tale. One of them, and it is a major book by a serious author and a very serious publisher, is called *Is There Anything Good About Men?* Another, by a legendary sociologist, is entitled *The Demise of Guys*. The third? *The End of Men: And the Rise of Women*.

It makes you want to weep.

There are many reasons for this crisis of manhood in our time, but I do not plan to spend much time describing them. It is not what we are here to do. It is also where a great many books and men's programs go wrong. They describe and analyze, mistaking conversation for meaningful change. They substitute words for action. It hasn't worked.

Please don't misunderstand me. I am not against words. I've written several dozen books myself. I'm also not against scholarship and cultural analysis. Both are part of what I do. Nor am I anti-intellectual. We need more serious thinking in our world, not less. We just do not need thought as a substitute for action. It's killing us.

In order to explain why I believe this to be true, I should define the four maxims that frame the vision of manhood I'm urging in these pages. They are the pillars upon which every other truth in this book rests, and they give meaning to the disciplines and virtues I'm asking men to incorporate into their lives. I think they are the four pillars of true manhood, the essentials for becoming manly men.

MANSFIELD'S
MANLY MAXIM #1

Someone once tried to summarize a principle in Aristotle's epic work *Poetics* with these words: "Action is character." Now Aristotle was describing the elements of drama when he wrote his *Poetics*, so he didn't necessarily mean what I mean here. Still, his basic premise is true: we know what a person's character is by what he does. I'm saying exactly the same thing, but I'm not referring to what happens on a stage. I'm referring to the life of a man.

I believe something fairly radical: true manhood comes from doing manly deeds. It is the mastery of a body of behaviors.

By words like *manly* and *manhood*, I don't mean the kind of behavior we see in the fake masculinity that surrounds us today. There's nothing manly about a guy downing booze until he throws up in the street. There's nothing manly about cruising for women like some predatory beast and then devouring them for pleasure before casting them aside. There's nothing manly about making a child but then running like a coward before that child is born. There's nothing manly about dominating a woman or treating her like a servant or leaving her with burdens that aren't rightly hers.

To think these actions make up true manhood is like thinking the average "gentlemen's club" is actually for gentlemen. It's not. Instead, it is a Palace of Perpetual Adolescence where incomplete males go to get on the cheap what they don't have the guts to fight for righteously and make their own.

Even the legitimate pleasures that men traditionally enjoy don't necessarily make them men. There certainly isn't anything uniquely manly about watching sports or smoking cigars or venturing into the wild or wearing the latest cut of suit or downing great gobs of food. None of these are inherently evil—I do all of them from time to time!—but none are inherently masculine, either.

Let's get this straight: none of this defines the kind of manhood I'm talking about here. I'm talking about the kind of manhood lived by bold, caring, principled, passionate men. I'm talking about the kind of manhood that makes a family whole, a woman safe, a child confident, and a community strong. I'm talking about a manhood rooted in heritage and honor and devotion to tribe. It is often rowdy and eager for fun, but it is always on duty and never fails to mind the borders of the territory it is assigned.

It is true, of course, that manhood like this usually grows from certain beliefs. But our society has discussed values and beliefs unceasingly. We've been like the football team that sits in the locker room and talks about how badly they are going to decimate the other team, but then never leaves the locker room to play the game. That locker room sure is a great place to hang out and talk smack! But it isn't the game. It isn't taking the field. That requires action.

Unfortunately, most of modern manhood is perpetually hanging out in the locker room—and talking, ever talking. Ultimately, though, you only know who a man is and what he believes by what he does. Not by what he sits around talking about. Not by what he says he feels. It's only when he acts—when he does something—that we start to know what he is.

Action is character. Manhood is action.

Some people are going to be uncomfortable with this conclusion. They'll want to say that true manhood comes from something else. A man becomes a true man by recovering his natural wildness. Or a man becomes a true man after he finds healing for his masculine soul. Or a man becomes a true man when he starts to resist being overdomesticated. Or a man becomes a true man by being like Jesus. Or Gandhi. Or Bono.

There is some truth in all of this.

Afterward, though—after the man starts following Jesus, or is liberated, or is healed, or is unleashed—how do we know he is a true man? We know only if he acts like one. If he behaves the way we know a man ought to behave. If he does the things men do.

The great mistake we have made in our generation is to think we can make a man with words. We need words, certainly. We just don't need words only. Yet by making words our primary tool in building men, we've talked the modern man to death. He is awash in a sea of words. He has language for things he hasn't even thought about doing—labels from a dozen therapeutic systems, lists and descriptions, and nifty slogans to keep him inspired. Fine. But has it made him a man? Has it made him act in noble, manly ways? Not usually. I think it has bored him to death. Or, worse, it has made him feel like a victim. Or, worse than that, it has made him feel understood, as though being understood is the meaning of life.

Here's the question: When does he start the doing? When does he act?

I think the more talk, the less action. I think the more drama, the less manhood. I also believe that the more talk, the more complex and unattainable manhood starts to seem to most men, particularly since the average man doesn't need that many words to begin with—on any subject!

Hear me, gentlemen: true men do things—manly things. Mere males who want to seem like men just talk. Manhood is in the doing.

There is a video on YouTube that I watch from time to time to remind me of this truth. As the video begins, a crowd has formed a circle at a sports facility and within that circle two fighters face each other. They have boxing gloves on, but you can tell they are about to engage in full-contact fighting. Both fighters warm up by doing great, arcing back kicks and impressive punch combinations. You inch up in your seat. You can tell this is going to be good.

The referee introduces the men and signals the start of the fight. One of the fighters is an impressive athlete. He keeps doing a type of forward, midair rotating kick that sends the crowd into delirium. He spins and spins. He's like a human rotor daring his opponent to step into the blades of his finely honed skills.

The other fighter looks to be in good shape, too, but he just bounces and jabs the air like every other fighter we've ever seen. You are pretty sure the first guy is going to kill this second guy, though.

Even after the referee signals the start, that first fighter keeps putting on a display of his spinning skill. He's amazing. The second fighter just watches, bounces and jabs the air.

Finally, as the first fighter is just in a spinner's mania, the crowd out of its mind with excitement, the second fighter takes two steps forward into the rotors and lands a punch on the other man's head just as that head is coming up from a spin. And the punch knocks our spinning fighter out cold. The second man waits a moment to be sure Blades of Death is really down for good. He is. Our second fighter then makes the universal "I Won/Touchdown" signal—both hands raised straight up into the air—and walks off. The fight is over.

Now that first fighter was an amazing athlete. He could sure spin.

He forgot, though, that fighters are supposed to fight. Dancing doesn't win fights. Fighting does.

I think it is the same with men. To be a man, you have to do man things. You can do other things, even woman things, but you won't be a man. A man does the things men do. It's how we know he is a man. It's how we benefit from what it means for him to be a man.

We'll flesh this out more in the pages to come, but for now take this down as Mansfield's Manly Maxim #1: *Manly men do manly things.*

> ## "MANHOOD AT THE MOST BASIC LEVEL CAN BE VALIDATED AND EXPRESSED ONLY IN ACTION."
> —*George Gilder, from* Sexual Suicide *(1973)*

MANSFIELD'S
MANLY MAXIM #2

OUR SECOND MAXIM IS SO IMPORTANT IT COULD ALMOST BE our only maxim. It's the key. It's the method. It's the vision. It's nearly the whole purpose for manhood. Little goes wrong when we live out this maxim. Almost everything goes wrong when we don't. In fact, the very first thing that went wrong in the world did so because the first man didn't live this truth.

Let me start with an illustration. I was a pretty good football player in my younger days. Because I was tall, strong, and fairly quick for my size, my coaches put me at defensive end. I had most of the skills I needed to play the position but, my friends, I definitely did not have the brain.

Once I figured out whom to hit or tackle, I could do the job. This important revelation seldom came to me until the man with the ball was well down the field. Let's just say my coaches were less than pleased. I ran a lot of laps after practice, did a lot of push-ups, and spent a lot of time listening to my coaches tell me things about my birth and my body parts that I did not know.

Fortunately, one of my coaches had played in the NFL, and he knew what to do. One day, in complete sputtering frustration, he grabbed the facemask of my helmet and dragged me to my place on the defensive line. Then, red faced and spitting mad, he said, "Listen, you *%!#*. I'm going to make it simple because you are so @*#!^# stupid! This," and he started dragging me along the perimeter of an imaginary box, "is your territory. No one, but no one, goes through this territory with the ball. Never, not once. If it ever happens I'm going to make you wish you'd never been born. Got it, you idiot?"

Coach could have used an anger management class or two, but he was a genius. I had been lost in trying to anticipate option plays and read "looks" and do unintelligible things like "string out the play." Do what with string? Coach made it simple. This is your territory. Own it. Guard its borders. Repel all invaders. Hunt down any threat and disarm it.

This I understood. This I could do. And I became a much better player. It helped that coach knew how to reinforce a lesson. When I failed to guard my territory in one particular game, he told me to meet him on the field early the following Monday morning before school. I arrived that morning in the dark and the cold—it was late November in Iowa. Coach met me and handed me scissors. He said he wanted me to "mow" the grass in my territory. He said I would probably guard it better if I took care of it. So I spent the next hour shivering on my knees and trying to see well enough to cut grass with scissors.

I cannot describe the difference this made in my simple little mind. I cut grass every morning of that school week, and I got to know every bare spot, rock and patch of grass in my territory. Because I knew it so well and suffered over it so miserably, I got protective—just what that sinister coach intended. He wanted me to own my part of the field, occupy my territory. I did. Frankly, I became a bit imbalanced. I discovered that I did not want anyone trampling on the blades of grass that had become my early-morning friends.

I started destroying running backs and splattering blockers who dared to sweep my way. Before long, I realized that the best way to keep the enemy from my territory was to hit the quarterback early and take away his ball. I did this often. I already possessed the strength and speed I needed long before coach turned me into a mental case. I just needed to understand my job and have some heartfelt reason for doing it. Defending my territory—and protecting my little grass buddies— proved reason enough.

Though this illustration might make you wonder if I'm sane, let me tell you it describes one of the defining features of genuine, effective manhood.

Listen up.

Every man has been given territory. Let's call it a field. It might help some men to think of it as a zone. This territory is defined by what a man is responsible for. The key to powerful manhood is that a man fully owns—takes responsibility for, tends, stands guard over, assures the healthy condition of—the field assigned to him.

When a man first starts out in the world, he may only be responsible for half a dorm room and a rusty car. He might also have a part-time job, schoolwork, and the care of body and soul to think about. These things make up his field. It's what he's responsible for. All of it. If he's a serious man who knows something of genuine manhood, he tends these things with zeal and devotion. They comprise the field assigned to him for this season of his life. And he knows that real men tend their fields.

His broader challenge is to learn to "man" his territory as a lifestyle. If he goes on a date, he understands he is responsible: not because his lady is weak and stupid, but because he asked her out and that, in the mind of a manly man, means he is responsible. He makes sure his date is safe. He makes sure he can do what he has promised to do—dinner and a movie, the horseback ride, the arrangements with friends—and he doesn't violate either her boundaries or the boundaries of God.

This sounds very "old school." It is. Get used to it. Being a real man in this generation is a great deal about recovering some old ways we should never have thrown aside.

So a man takes responsibility for his field—even if this field is only a dorm room, an old clunky car, a suitcase of clothes, his studies, and an occasional date. He mans his zone because he knows it is his job as a man. He also knows, though, that when a man tends his field, it leads to a bigger field.

If our young man tends this first field well, he may eventually have a wife, a home, and meaningful work to do. Then, perhaps, there will be children, increased income to manage, and a role to fulfill in the community. He doesn't resent these duties. He mans his zone out of love for those who have been entrusted to him and the calling of God. He takes responsibility for the field assigned to him because he knows this is what he is put on earth to do. He also knows that faithfulness now is the key to increase later. So he guards and nurtures what he's assigned. In time, who knows? His art impacts a larger audience. His message is more widely heard. He influences more hearts and minds. Maybe he's entrusted with managing a city. Or guiding a church. Or leading a nation.

Man your territory. It's what men do. It's how men love. It's also how increase comes.

The great male failing is just the opposite: neglect. You can picture the scene. A man sits in his recliner wearing a stained T-shirt and sweat pants, TV remote and beer in hand. He hardly moves. All weekend. He sends the kids to the kitchen to get his next beer, and he bellows for his wife to make a sandwich before the third quarter starts. This guy feels entitled. He works hard at the plant or in the office. Doing nothing in front of the TV is his reward.

His field needs tending, though. His wife is hurting and exhausted. She's also put on weight and is starting to limp. His daughter is almost never home and is becoming increasingly protective of her privacy—and whatever that is in her purse. His son is awkward and pimply and growing resentful. He spends more and more of his time locked away in his room.

The house could be lovely but for a few hundred small repairs. The family hasn't laughed together or even had an uninterrupted meal in months, and the yard is so horrible the neighbors walk by shaking their heads. This family used to go to church together and talk about important things. They used to do family projects to make money for their beach trip each summer. They used to serve at the homeless shelter.

Now only harsh, resentful words pass between them. Money is tight. Each life reveals its deepening damage. The man and his wife have not touched each other in years.

This is an extreme example, perhaps, but I'm describing a family I know. I also know that as the man squeezes his blubber into his Barcalounger, he grumbles that his son won't do the yard and his daughter won't clean the house and his wife won't cook a decent meal and be ready in bed. Typically, he blames. He accuses. He gripes. He's angry.

The key to change is in his hands. All of these things are happening on his watch. He's responsible. He doesn't own the lives in his home, but he is responsible for them—for their spiritual health and their moral rectitude and their sense of what they are made to be. He's responsible to provide for them, of course, but also to nurture them, coach them, and help them fulfill their purpose in this life. He does not have to do everything, but he is responsible to make sure everything gets done—the tending of hearts and minds first, then guaranteeing a home of love and encouragement, and finally fashioning the physical part of his territory so it makes noble living possible.

It is all his to guard and cultivate, to watch over and maintain.

If he would man his territory, he would reap great rewards, particularly in the hearts of those he says he loves. Instead, his meager reward is a beer, a badly made sandwich, an embittered family, and a life in decline.

Here is the big picture: it is the job of a man to know the definition of the field assigned to him. Who "belongs" to him? What is he responsible for? What boundaries is he guarding? What forces—physical, moral, emotional, spiritual, intellectual—must he guard against? What needs to be done? And, certainly, what does God require?

Then, having answered these questions, it is the job of a man to cultivate that field—to guard its boundaries, assure its health, provide for it generously, and fill it with love so it thrives.

There is far more to say about this, but for now let's sum it up in Mansfield's Manly Maxim #2: *Manly men tend their fields.*

"BIG JOBS USUALLY GO TO THE MEN WHO PROVE THEIR ABILITY TO OUTGROW SMALL ONES."

—*Theodore Roosevelt, quoted in* The Management Review, *vol. 6, American Management Association (1919)*

MANSFIELD'S
MANLY MAXIM #3

MANLY MAXIM #3 IS VITALLY IMPORTANT, BUT GIVE ME A minute to work my way to it. I have a story to tell that will help us.

Not long ago, I changed from what we'll call Computer System B to what we'll call Computer System A. Now during all the years I used Computer System B, my biggest challenge was learning what I needed to know. When I bought the computer and turned it on, it just stared at me, blinking. I had to go get a book and read. I did what the book told me to do, and the computer started doing a few things. When I wanted the computer to do more things, and I installed a new piece of software, I had to go get another book and learn how that new software worked too. In fact, I sometimes had to go get a book about why the second piece of software had messed up the software that was already on the computer. Since different companies made the two pieces of software, their products didn't necessarily play well together. The same thing happened when I added some cool new piece of hardware. More books. More arguing technologies. More books about how books on arguing technologies don't tell you everything you need to know.

Finally, after enduring many hours of me in a grumbling, techno-ticked mood, my amazing wife, Beverly, decided to make a change. She was a longtime user of Computer System A and she knew what I was missing.

One day, she ripped all of Computer System B out of my life: every piece of squabbling software and misbehaving hardware—along with the dozens of books they required—and she gave me the notebook computer and the smartphone of Computer System A.

I can hardly find the words to describe what came next. Let's just say there was a fit. I turned on the computer and everything I needed was just there. Every time I did something, what I needed to do next was pretty obvious. Someone had already thought it through and made the way to do it simple.

After a while, I realized something important was happening. It wasn't the technological revolution I was experiencing, as astounding as this new system was. It was an educational revolution. I never opened a book. I never took a class. I don't recall even consulting a website. I became a fairly sophisticated user of Computer System A all by either doing or by learning from people around me. In fact, I got good enough to teach others, having never opened a book. Doing and the example of others made me more effective than I had ever been. Doing and the example of others.

It occurred to me later that this is how I had learned most of the things that defined my life. For example, I became a pretty good foot-ball player in my early life. I'm not saying I was God's gift to the NFL, but I was pretty good. How did I get that way? Doing and the example of others. Perhaps some coaching. No books. No seminars. No long lectures. Someone did. I watched. Then I did. Over time, I did better. That was it. It's just how I later learned Computer System A. It's also how, early on in my life, I learned how to drive, date, mow grass, study, find my way to the best pizza place, and dress in really cool and exotic ways. On the dark side, it's also how I learned to lie, fight, steal, cuss, and hide porn. The point, though, is that doing and the example of others is how I learned most everything that shaped my life.

This may be how all human beings learn best, but it is certainly the way most men learn what matters: doing and the example of others. Yet, oddly, when society wants men to be better men, it gives them books and sends them to classes. This has given us male spectators. It has not given us better men.

I remember some years ago I was listening to an African bishop describe the wonderful things his churches were doing in a difficult part of his country. Hundreds of us listened to him, and we were deeply moved. After he spoke, the bishop took questions. Someone asked what a great many of us wanted to know: Why aren't things like you describe happening here in our country?

The man wasn't a diplomat. I liked that about him, and I liked it more after he answered this question. He said, "Here is the reason you do not have such things happening in this country. You Americans study your God. We Africans worship ours. You get smarter. We get changed. And then we change the world around us."

I thought the audience was going to riot. The bishop wasn't finished, though. His next words never left me. "By doing rather than merely studying, we create a culture. Newcomers and the young feed on that culture. They watch. They do. They, too, are changed. Our culture expands. You Americans create a system of thought. The most you ask is that people contemplate new ideas. You might ask them to give or to sometimes attend meetings, but no contagious culture is created. Nothing is offered to newcomers and the young but thoughts. So they think. They don't do."

We are changed. We craft a contagious culture. People feed on this culture and change the world.

I believe it is exactly the same with the making of men. We can inspire and teach men with study—with words, books, and classes. We can only make men, though, in the contagious culture created by other genuine men.

The good news is this happens naturally. Put a young, unformed man in the presence of older men, and the process automatically begins. It is simply the outworking of the way men are made. The young man watches. He listens. He ponders. Soon, he becomes what he beholds. He starts patterning himself, almost without intending to, after these impressive older men. This can happen without the older men intentionally teaching a lesson or addressing the younger man directly. It is a result of the contagious power of genuine manhood and the way men intuitively absorb the manly culture around them.

I had few mentors when I was young. My father was relatively distant and often away on assignment. I did have coaches and teachers who left their imprint, but my father's military career meant that we moved to a new post almost every year. No one had the opportunity to shape me for very long.

When I finished college and moved to West Texas, I started spending time with some older men who had lived in that area all their lives. They were cowboys, really: I mean real, hat-wearing, cow-herding cowboys who carried pistols on their hips and rifles in their pickup truck windows. These men ended up providing some of the male mentoring I lacked in my life.

Don't misunderstand. They hardly said anything directly to me. Most of them thought I was a citified Yankee who wasn't worth speaking to.

Still, they had a way of talking that helped me. They used sentences like, "Well, if Joe was any kind of man he would do such and such." Or, they'd say, "Seems to me a man'd have a talk with that ol' boy who was causin' so much trouble." Then there was my favorite. It was like code. One guy would turn to the other and say, "A man'd know what to do."

This usually meant that something had happened and that there was a "feller" who needed to be put up against a wall and told how the world works. We just weren't going to mention such things in front of the ladies. All the men understood, though: "A man'd know what to do."

The point is these grizzled Texans taught me, whether they wanted to or not. It's how man culture works. I also learned from that teacher who caught me in a lie and said, "When you're man enough, come back and tell me the truth." Then there was that coach who was gracious and polite to women and yet always careful not to leave the wrong impression. I noticed. I thought about it. I learned.

I learned also from my linebacker friend who saw a man yelling at his wife in the mall. My friend—six-foot, four inches tall and 240 pounds of stone muscle—walked over and just put his finger in the man's chest. That's all. Didn't say a word. He just stood there and radiated: "This is wrong. Stop. Now. Or else."

I learned. Manhood. Lesson #42.

I learned also from my pastor's prayers and my father's Southern manners and the way a policeman once dealt with a woman in a drunken rage and from an older friend who said, "You're better than that" when I was demonstrating my finely honed cussing skills.

I even learned from a man in my church who said exactly two words to me. It had snowed heavily where I lived then and the man came by my house at six the morning after. When I opened the door he said, "Come on." That's it. Nothing more. I put on my coat and got in his truck. We started driving around town checking on the elderly. We shoveled snow. We adjusted their heaters. We made sure they had food. The old man wasn't mean. He was on a mission. It is what men do. They take care of their people. *Shut up, young man. Get to it. The old ones are waiting and afraid.*

I got it. I also got that manly culture doesn't require much more than one genuine man living a noble life before other men. It reminds me of a story they often tell in Texas. They revere the Texas Rangers there—the lawmen, not the baseball team. In the frontier days, there was a riot in a particular town and the mayor of that town frantically called for the Texas Rangers. One Ranger showed up. The mayor couldn't believe it. "One Ranger? What in the world are you guys thinking! We need help!" The Ranger picked his teeth for a moment and then said, "Yes, one Ranger. There's only one riot, isn't there?" Then he ended the riot. Texans walk around to this day reminding each other: "One riot. One Ranger."

The same is true with men as a whole. All it takes for a contagious manly culture to form is for one genuine man to live out genuine manhood. It creates a model, something for other men to feed upon and pattern themselves after. It also gives other genuine men a vital connection that sustains and extends who they are.

This, then, is Mansfield's Manly Maxim #3: *Manly men build manly men.*

> ## "A WOMAN SIMPLY IS, BUT A MAN MUST BECOME. MASCULINITY IS RISKY AND ELUSIVE . . . AND IT IS CONFIRMED ONLY BY OTHER MEN."
>
> —*Camille Paglia, from* Sex, Art and American Culture: New Essays *(1992)*

A REAL MAN

Men are of two kinds, and he
Was of the kind I'd like to be.
Some preach their virtues, and a few
Express their lives by what they do.
That sort was he. No flowery phrase
Or glibly spoken words of praise
Won friends for him. He wasn't cheap
Or shallow, but his course ran deep,
And it was pure. You know the kind.
Not many in a life you find
Whose deeds outrun their words so far
That more than what they seem they are.

There are two kinds of lies as well:
The kind you live, the ones you tell.
Back through his years from age to youth
He never acted one untruth.
Out in the open light he fought
And didn't care what others thought
Nor what they said about his fight
If he believed that he was right.
The only deeds he ever hid
Were acts of kindness that he did.

What speech he had was plain and blunt.
His was an unattractive front.
Yet children loved him; babe and boy
Played with the strength he could employ,
Without one fear, and they are fleet

To sense injustice and deceit.
No back door gossip linked his name
With any shady tale of shame.
He did not have to compromise
With evil-doers, shrewd and wise,
And let them ply their vicious trade
Because of some past escapade.

Men are of two kinds, and he
Was of the kind I'd like to be.
No door at which he ever knocked
Against his manly form was locked.
If ever man on earth was free
And independent, it was he.
No broken pledge lost him respect,
He met all men with head erect,
And when he passed, I think there went
A soul to yonder firmament
So white, so splendid and so fine
It came almost to God's design.

—EDGAR A. GUEST

MANSFIELD'S
MANLY MAXIM #4

I HAVE SAID THUS FAR "MANLY MEN DO MANLY THINGS." I have said, "Manly men tend their fields." I have also said, "Manly men make manly men."

These are all true and they are all essential to genuine manhood. They are not possible, though, without our final maxim. It is this: *"Manly men live to the glory of God."*

I believe that a man's purpose in this world is so unique, that it is meant to be one of such service and sacrifice, that he cannot fulfill his role successfully without doing so to the glory of God. There are many reasons for this.

First, a man cannot fulfill his purpose if he is living for applause, approval, and affirmation in this world. It simply will not come—not enough, certainly, to answer the needs of his soul.

If a man lives for the glory of God, he stops looking for affirmation from other human beings after every good deed, a pat on the head every time he does his duty. Instead, he throws himself into his role unselfishly. He contents himself with knowing he is fulfilling his purpose in this world and pleasing the God who made him. His reward comes when he is able to say, as we heard the Scottish Olympian and missionary Eric Liddell say in *Chariots of Fire*, "When I run, I feel his pleasure."

Second, a man is meant to carry such responsibility that he will descend into exhaustion and resentment if he does not have the inner resources that come from living in connection with God. This is much the same for women, but that is the subject for another book by another author. The issue for men is, as much as they might try, they cannot do what they are assigned to do without strength and energy beyond their own. This comes from being men to the glory of God.

Third, men are meant to tend the lives of others in such a way that they must have insight that comes from beyond them. I've often suspected that my wife, a woman of great wisdom, simply has a resident gift. In other words, her insight and understanding live in her permanently, it seems. She's always wise and always aware of what to do. She's usually right. I'm not as gifted. I have to ask God constantly for understanding and insight that do not live in me day to day. In my life, this comes from living to the glory of God.

Finally, what I am saying of manly men is only what is true for all of life. Human beings are made by God and are made to live in relationship with God. It is the only way we will ever be whole or fulfilled or empowered or effective. It is also the only way we can be the unique creatures we are called to be. I am a husband, a father, a teacher, a writer, a leader, and an entrepreneur. Each of these roles has its source and its fuel in God. He is all these things and millions of others besides. Stephen Mansfield cannot be what he is made to be on his own. Everything he is designed for draws power in the most immediate and personal sense from God. This isn't just true of me or of men. It is true of all of creation.

Someone will inevitably ask me if I'm saying that a man who doesn't believe in God cannot be a good man. No, that's not what I'm saying—although the problem is defining the word *good*.

I strive to be a good man as I see *good man* described in Scripture and in the example of Jesus Christ, whom I believe to be the perfect man, the model for all men.

I have friends, though, who believe they are good men and good husbands because they have large muscles and keep their wives amply supplied with expensive clothes and vacations. I have friends who believe they are good because their wives are "allowed" to work outside the home. I have friends who believe they are good because they do not beat their wives as their fathers did. I have friends who believe they are good because they feel deep affection for their wives and spend quality time with them every day. I know one man who thinks he is a good man because he lets his wife take other men for lovers.

Each of these men thinks himself good by some definition. Each has a system of belief that defines for him what it means to be a man. You see the problem? What definition of good and of manhood should we live by? I believe it ought to be God's definition as found in Scripture and the teachings of Jesus. I'm not smart enough to craft a definition of my own. Some of my friends have crafted their own definitions, as you can see, but what they've come up with looks like folly to me.

I keep it simple. I can't live up to God's standards without God's resources. I become the man I am made to be by living to the glory of God.

This gives us Mansfield's Manly Maxim #4: *Manly men live to the glory of God.*

"HAVING THUS CHOSEN OUR COURSE,
WITHOUT GUILES AND WITH PURE
PURPOSE, LET US RENEW OUR TRUST
IN GOD, AND GO FORWARD WITHOUT
FEAR AND WITH MANLY HEARTS."

—*Abraham Lincoln, Address to Congress, July 4, 1861*

THE FOUR MANLY MAXIMS

These, then, are Mansfield's Manly Maxims:

> 1. MANLY MEN DO MANLY THINGS.
> 2. MANLY MEN TEND THEIR FIELDS.
> 3. MANLY MEN BUILD MANLY MEN.
> 4. MANLY MEN LIVE TO THE GLORY OF GOD.

These are more than just my personal maxims. They are pillars of a house of genuine manhood that urgently needs to be rebuilt in our time. Read them. Ponder them. Pray them. Absorb them from the great lives we are about to see. Remember, though, that it is only by doing these maxims that they will become reality in your life.

In the *Nicomachean Ethics* Aristotle said, "Men acquire a particular quality by constantly acting a particular way . . . you become just by performing just actions, temperate by performing temperate actions, brave by performing brave actions."

This is also the way we become manly men!

THE MANLY MAN

The World has room for the manly man, with the
   spirit of manly cheer;
The world delights in the man who smiles when his
   eyes keep back the tear;
It loves the man who, when things are wrong, can take
   his place and stand
With his face to the fight and his eyes to the light, and
   toil with a willing hand;
The manly man is the country's need, the moment's
   need, forsooth,
With a heart that beats to the pulsing troop of the
   lilied leagues of truth;
The world is his and it waits for him, and it leaps to
   hear the ring
Of the blow he strikes and the wheels he turns and
   hammers he dares to swing;
It likes the forward look on his face, the poise of his
   noble head,
And the onward lunge of his tireless will and the sweep
   of his dauntless tread!
Hurrah for the manly man who comes with sunlight
   on his face,
And the strength to do and the will to dare and the
   courage to find his place!
The world delights in the manly man, and the weak
   and evil flee
When the manly man goes forth to hold his own on
   land or sea!

—AUTHOR UNKNOWN

42

PART TWO

Show me the man you honor, and I will know what kind of man you are, for it shows me what your ideal of manhood is and what kind of man you long to be.

—Thomas Carlyle, from Latter-day Pamphlets, *no. 07, Hudson's Statue, July 1850*

If you know history, you know that there is no such thing as a self-made man or self-made woman. We are shaped by people we have never met.

—David McCullough, from "The Course of Human Events," Jefferson Lecture, National Endowment for the Humanities, 2003

If a man does not have an ideal and try to live up to it, then he becomes a mean, base and sordid creature, no matter how successful.

—Theodore Roosevelt, in a letter to his son Kermit on January 27, 1915, as published in Theodore Roosevelt and his time: Shown in his own letters, vol. 1, *by Joseph B. Bishop (1920)*

SHOW YOURSELF A MAN

As David, king of Israel, prepared to pass from this life sometime around the year 970 BC, he called his son Solomon to his side and spoke his final words. This is how he began: "I am about to go the way of all the earth. Be strong, and show yourself a man" (1 Kings 2:2 ESV).

The king was not telling his son to be a male. That would have been unnecessary. Instead, he was charging his son to be all that it means to be a man of God, to be—as we are saying with a wink in this book—a manly man. The words for *show yourself a man* in Hebrew mean something like "become what it means to be an exceptional man."

The original word *show* helps us, though, because it puts the emphasis on the idea of doing, of demonstrating or living out the characteristics of manhood. The focus of David's words, as with the focus of this book, is upon the doing, upon being sure to "show" the behavior of a genuine man.

While we read the brief stories of great men that follow in these pages, we never want to forget King David's challenge. We want ultimately to arrive at the question of how we will live differently because of what we have read. Otherwise, we might be tempted to enjoy these stirring tales as entertainment without allowing them to make us better men.

To help seal the meaning of these stories into our lives, we will end each one with these words: *What then will you do? How will you show yourself a man?* These questions will be followed by more questions and a variety of prompts to guide us in living out the meaning of what we have read.

Let these words, then, burn themselves into your mind: *In light of what I've learned, how will I show myself a man?*

A MAN

A man doesn't whine at his losses.
A man doesn't whimper and fret,
Or rail at the weight of his crosses
And ask life to rear him a pet.
A man doesn't grudgingly labor
Or look upon toil as a blight;
A man doesn't sneer at his neighbor
Or sneak from a cause that is right.

A man doesn't sulk when another
Succeeds where his efforts have failed;
Doesn't keep all his praise for the brother
Whose glory is publicly hailed;
And pass by the weak and the humble
As though they were not of his clay;
A man doesn't ceaselessly grumble
When things are not going his way.

A man looks on woman as tender
And gentle, and stands at her side
At all times to guard and defend her,
And never to scorn or deride.
A man looks on life as a mission.
To serve, just so far as he can;
A man holds his noblest ambition
On earth is to live as a man.

—EDGAR A. GUEST

HONOR

Most of the men I describe in this book are famous, though the stories I tell about them may not be. Occasionally, I intend to tell the story of a man who is relatively obscure. This is for two reasons. First, I want us to learn to absorb the lessons of manly greatness wherever we find them, in the famous as well as the unknown. Second, I want to make sure we understand that genuine manliness is its own reward and that it has little to do with fame or the attention of history.

Our first man in the "relatively unknown" category is a bit of an oddity. We don't know much about him. He appears only once in the pages of history and only in a document that dates from sometime around the fifth century BC. This single reference is a mere five sentences long and it pertains to the man's early life, perhaps his teen years. We know his tribe, but we do not know his father. We know the personality of his mother but we do not know her name. We know he had brothers but we know only one thing about them: they were not as honorable as he was. And this is where the story begins.

We are introduced to this man simply. He was, we are told, "more honorable than his brothers." This statement comes as a break in a mind-numbingly long list of names. This was how lessons were announced in the genealogies of the ancient world. To draw attention, you injected your subject suddenly, your first line read as though you had been discussing the matter for hours, and you stated the theme of your lesson right at the beginning. In this case, the theme is that our man is honorable, "more honorable than his brothers."

The subject is announced, then. Here comes a lesson in honor.

The very next statement is an explanation of how our man got his name. Apparently, his mother named her son after a bad experience she had when he was born.

Again, in the style of ancient narratives, this is a signal. There's more here than merely an explanation of the man's name. This is said to give us insight into his life. The writer assumes he doesn't have to say much because we are going to think hard about what little he does say. And what the writer says points directly to our man's mother.

Mom is the key to this story. She is apparently the kind of woman who builds monuments to her disappointment with life in the souls of her children. We are told she named her son with the word in her language that meant "pain" and she did it because she had endured pain when he was born. Think about this. She did not name her son something noble or inspiring, but rather a word that would remind him all his life of how his mother suffered when he was born. Every time he was called to dinner, every time his friends yelled out to him, he was reminded that he caused his mother pain when he was born.

A woman willing to brand her son with her sufferings is a woman who will mention her hardships whenever they can be of use. So it is not difficult to imagine this mother saying, "Oh, so you didn't clean your room, huh? Don't you remember the pain you caused me when you were born? Don't you care that I suffered?"

The very first sentence of this little tale tells us that our man had brothers. So who knows what they were named! I've got friends whose Cherokee names mean "rabbit run in snow" or "deer eat apple," because these things happened on the day they were born. Perhaps our man's brothers were called "Bedpan Too Cold" or "Doctor Bill Too Big." It would fit. Whatever this woman endured, she burned into the lives of her children by the way she named them.

Think about a home filled with this bitter, backward-looking spirit. We've all been with people who couldn't ask for the salt at a meal without leaking the bitterness that permeated their lives. This is what our man's home was like. People rehearsed their disillusionment and recounted their fears. They told stories to convince themselves of their curses and scoffed at the idea that the future could be any different from their horrible past.

They were living a postage stamp existence. Whatever their physical space, their spiritual space was nearly microscopic. There was no vision, no sense of the possibilities of life. No one told inspiring stories or mentioned the miraculous things happening in the world or devoted a single word to igniting heroic purposes in someone else's soul. No. There was life. It was hard. We should never forget. It would always be this way.

But our man—his name was Yabetz, by the way—was suffocating. Having lived for many years in a home with small-minded, backward-looking people, he felt like a man being crushed to death.

There's more. We all know what happens to people who think about the evils that have befallen them, worry about more evil befalling them, and who are convinced of befalling evil yet to fall. Yes, that's it: evil befalls them. They become pain magnets. Damage and loss fill their days. Their reality is confirmation of their fears. This is how Yabetz's family, dominated by his bitter, disillusioned mother, lived out their days.

But not all of them. The reason that this story is even worth telling is because of something Yabetz did. One day, he had simply endured all he could. He wasn't going to live this way anymore.

He went and stood before his God and prayed this: "Oh, that you would bless me and enlarge my territory! Let your hand be with me, and keep me from harm so that I will be free from pain." And the last words of this five-sentence story in the middle of an ancient document tell us that God answered his request.

Look at that prayer carefully. Every word is important. For some reason this man Yabetz has realized that there is a destructive process at work in his life. He's decided to push back. He realizes there is a curse pressing itself into his life, and he knows it has the power to destroy him.

So Yabetz cries out, *"Oh that you would bless me . . ."*

Then our man realizes this curse has robbed him and his people. Not only are they small in spirit and dim of vision, but also much good that should have been theirs was taken from them. Or lost by their own folly. So they live out a smallness of soul that keeps them small in every way.

So Yabetz cries out, *"Enlarge my territory."*

He also realizes it will take an act of God to free him from the grip of this thing that is crushing him.

So Yabetz cries out, *"Let your hand be with me."*

This is important symbolic language in Yabetz's time. Whenever his God does something magnificent, the prophets and wise men say the "hand of God" has done such and such. Yabetz makes this symbolism part of his prayer.

Finally, he locates his target and sends the words of his prayer right into the heart of it: *"Keep me from harm and free me from pain."*

There it is. Remember now: Yabetz's name means pain. It is the curse his mother put upon him when he was born. That word has defined Yabetz all his days. He understands this all too well, and he wants the power of this word cancelled in his life: "Free me from pain." *Free me from the curse of my name. Free me from the curse of my people's ways. Free me from smallness and loss and living like a wounded animal and seeing only the ugly and the dark. Free me from this suffocating spirit and make me what you have ordained, O God.*

And God did, we are told.

But that's all we know. That's it. There's no more to it. The next words in this ancient document have nothing to do with this startling story. In fact, the list of names just drones on: "Kelub, Shuhah's brother, was the father of Mehir, who was the father of Eshrton. Eshrton was the father of Beth Rapha . . ." And so it goes, page after page. There had already been entire chapters of this kind before our man Yabetz was even mentioned.

Very strange. But there is something about this story, isn't there? It stirs us. There is something that draws us to this tale of a man seeking to be free from the constrictions and dysfunctions that have defined his life. We feel kinship with him. His story calls to us.

There is one more fact that may help us flesh out this man's life and allow us to understand its magnetic pull on our hearts. You see, the big question is, "How did Yabetz begin to envision something more?" What made him think he could be free, that there was a life outside of what he had always known? Most people raised in bitterness and nurtured in disillusionment never change. The wounded seem to live on in perpetual retreat. The offended seem ever in wait for somebody to set things right. Seldom do tainted souls break out of the pattern of years. They can't see beyond their experience, can't envision a life beyond the curse.

Yabetz did. But why? How?

I'll tell you what I think but this is a good moment to remind you that the theme of this story is not anything we are talking about right now. It isn't blessing or pain or contentious mothers or the trauma of birth. It is honor. Remember? "And Yabetz was more *honorable* than his brothers."

Hold on to this and let me tell you what I think has happened to our young friend from centuries ago. The only other fact we know about Yabetz is that he was part of a tribe named Yehuda, and Yehuda was the son of the founder of Yabetz's tribe.

When this founder was dying, he gave a blessing—words of spiritual power and vision—to his son Yehuda, just as he did to each of his other sons. But the blessing he gave to Yehuda was particularly awe-inspiring. The tribal founder said that Yehuda would be lionlike and that he would carry both a royal scepter and a ruler's staff in his hands. Nations would bow to him. He would be victorious over his enemies, walk in favor with his brothers and be prosperous. There is even some indication that he would be handsome.

This was the founding blessing of Yabetz's tribe. These words were sacred—to all the tribes but to the descendants of Yehuda in particular. Priests, wise men, and bards would have recounted this blessing in holy rituals, when the heritage of the tribe was celebrated and when the people were tempted to forget who they were.

Picture Yabetz with me. He is in his late teens or early twenties. He's a bit insecure. He has a somewhat lonely, slightly haunted look on his face. One evening, members of his tribe gather around a fire and the storytellers and priests start recounting the lore of the tribe. Yabetz squeezes in between two elders. He hears the stories. He's stirred. He laughs. He hears of heroes past for the hundredth time, but their adventures never seem to lose their thrill. Then one of the elders or perhaps a priest sees the need to recount the founding blessing of the tribe before the evening is done.

Yabetz has heard the words many times before. He knows them by heart. Every member of the tribe does. On this night, they fill the air again. *Lionlike. The scepter and the staff. Nations shall bow. Enemies defeated.*

There is nothing new, and yet on this night as I imagine it, the words explode in Yabetz's heart. He is living in an oppressive home, filled with sorrow, bitterness, and regret. The grief and the fear choke him. He feels he is dying, that a spirit of smallness and pain has taken him by the throat.

Then the words, the ones spoken in that blessing centuries before. And suddenly Yabetz sees. The words unveil themselves inside of him as they never have before. He need not be defined by his family's poisonous ways. There is a greater heritage that can shape his life.

He does not have to live craven and resentful. He is called to lion-like ways. He need not live wounded and harmed. He is meant to rule, to stalk his prey and conquer his enemies. He need not live cursed and hated. He is among a people destined for favor.

Yabetz sees the heritage he has by virtue of faith and belonging to a people, a heritage his biology and family culture would embed in him. He chooses. And then he cries out to the only one who can make the words of the blessing come to pass. "Oh, that you would bless me . . ."

And Yabetz is freed, because a loving God—who put this blessing in the mouth of the tribe's founder in the first place—hears and responds.

We come, then, to the heart of the matter, gentlemen: the reason we have begun with this age-old story. Remember the word *honor*? We were told that Yabetz was more honorable than his brothers. Why? Certainly what has happened to Yabetz is thrilling, but why is he more honorable than his brothers? Why is he even mentioned in the middle of this otherwise dull administrative record while his brothers are never even named?

I believe it is because honor is a temper of heart, a quality of spirit, a cast of soul that refuses the oppressive, the petty, and the unclean in order to reach instead to what God has intended: nobility, abundance, and strength. Yabetz reached beyond his bitter conditioning and took hold of his loftier, grander, destined self. God calls this honor.

Notice that Yabetz's brothers heard the same words Yabetz did.

They had the same opportunity, the same heritage, the same destiny by faith. They did not grasp it for themselves. They did not echo Yabetz's plea before God. They were, then, less honorable, we are told.

Men, this is where we start. Like Yabetz, we, too, have wounds and regrets, curses and smallness. We, too, have voices in our lives that reinforce fear and despair. We might also have a growing sense that we are less than what we were made to be. Our wounds and failures make us cower in the shadows while our wives, our sons and daughters, and those we are meant to protect and lead suffer from our refusal to be—honorable. Like Yabetz.

Bless me. Enlarge me. Free me from the curse of what I have been. Let your hand be upon me.

The core lesson comes to us fiery and fast. Honorable men refuse to wallow in the small and the bitter. Honorable men refuse to hate life because something once went wrong. Honorable men don't build monuments to their disappointments, nor do they let others brand them and curse them to their destruction.

Honorable men seek out the highest definition of their lives, the nobler meaning granted by heritage, by their ancestors' dreams and their parents' hopes. Honorable men cry out to God until curses are broken and a grander purpose is achieved. Honorable men don't settle for lives of regret.

I imagine you have already figured out what I have done here. Yabetz is the Hebrew name for *Jabez*. You have likely heard this name before. It comes from the story I have told as it appears in 1 Chronicles 4:9–11, a passage from the Old Testament. Yehuda, of course, is the Hebrew pronunciation of *Judah*. And Judah's father was Jacob—also known as Israel, the man after whom the modern nation is named.

I changed these names slightly to give you a chance to hear this story as though for the first time. It is more than a mere Bible story that perhaps you first heard in Sunday school years ago. It is a tale of what God will do in the lives of men who reach for honor. I didn't want you to miss this potential simply because you have heard some of this before.

WHAT THEN WILL YOU DO?
HOW WILL YOU SHOW YOURSELF A MAN?

1. What does your name mean? Is there any clue to your parents' hopes, or even God's intentions, in the meaning of your name in its original language?
2. What words were said about your life when you were born? Form these words of blessing and vision into prayers and destinations. Make curses and negative labels into Yabetz-like prayers.
3. What tribe do you belong to? Is there any defining language or story that comes with belonging to that tribe? Take them for yourself. Make them a matter of prayer. Live their ideals. If some of the words that swirl around your tribe are negative, do as Yabetz did: ask God to break the curse and enlarge you.
4. Take a loving, honest look at your family culture. Take the good and extend it. Identify the harsh, the bitter, and the destructive and work against it. Do this in prayer, in discipline, and by living in exactly the opposite spirit.
5. Consider keeping an "Honor Book" or some "Honor Pages" in your journal if you already use one. Record the words that nobly define your life: words of your ancestors, tribal leaders, parents, teachers, coaches, friends, and so on. Record words from Scripture, poems, books, even movies and songs that embedded themselves in you when you heard them and have become part of who you are and want to be. Rehearse them, make them yours, pray them, ask God to break the opposite

of these noble words in your life, and celebrate on the page your journey into honor. Don't feel silly or unmanly about this. George Washington, George Patton, Ronald Reagan, and some of the greatest men who ever lived did this too!

"NOTHING GREAT WILL EVER BE ACHIEVED WITHOUT GREAT MEN, AND MEN ARE GREAT ONLY IF THEY ARE DETERMINED TO BE SO. FOR GLORY GIVES HERSELF ONLY TO THOSE WHO HAVE ALWAYS DREAMED OF HER."

—*Charles De Gaulle, from* The Army of the Future (Vers l'armée de métier), *1941*

LEGACY

It was late in 1964 when a letter arrived at a London townhouse. The nine-year-old girl in Colombia, South America, who mailed the letter had done so without including a stamp or a complete address. Nevertheless, the postal service in Colombia had known just what to do. Workers there provided the missing stamp and sent the letter on its way. It arrived in England a few days later, where workers immediately sent it to 28 Hyde Park Gate in London. A secretary then opened the envelope, read the note inside, and handed it to a ninety-year-old gentleman sitting nearby. He smiled, grateful and amused. His name was Winston Churchill. The letter was addressed simply, "To the Greatest Man in the World."

Winston Churchill was indeed the greatest man of his age. His life was astonishingly rich and productive. His gifts were measured in the gratitude of millions. His impact upon his world cannot be fully measured yet. It must be left to generations yet unborn.

He came into the world in 1874. There were men still living who had fought Napoleon. Abraham Lincoln had been president just nine years before. He grew up one of two sons of the American beauty Jennie Jerome and Lord Randolph Churchill, rising statesman and noted champion of Tory democracy.

His parents were typical of their day and left young Winston in the care of a nanny named Elizabeth Everest. This was fortunate. She gave him the love his parents were incapable of and led him gently to an understanding of the ways of God. She also embedded in him a sense of destiny that never left him.

He attended Sandhurst, the British military academy, and soon after found himself in the crossfire of battle in the Sudan, in Cuba, in India, and, finally, in the Boer War of South Africa, where he was captured and held as a prisoner of war. His escape made him world famous, and he parlayed this into a successful run for Parliament. His fortunes would rise and fall in British politics, but it was obvious to friends that he was being fashioned for a role beyond mere political infighter.

He served as first lord of the admiralty during World War I but resigned when his planned invasion of Turkey through the Dardanelles proved disastrous and resulted in the deaths of more than one hundred thousand men. He led soldiers in Belgium, returned to politics after the war, and then became an outcast in British society because of his impassioned warnings about the Nazi rise in Germany. England was weary of war, having lost a generation of young men in the trenches of World War I. Churchill seemed a shrill warmonger. He became one of the most hated men in Britain.

In the late 1930s, many of his predictions proved true. As the Nazis began marching through Europe, Churchill returned as first lord of the admiralty and then, when no amount of appeasement would make Hitler stand down, was summoned by the king to serve as prime minister. It was a terrible time in history, and many commentators predicted the end of the Western democracies. Churchill saw the threat but believed in his nation, his God, and his own destined purpose. A coalition inspired in part by Churchill's moral fire finally prevailed in 1945.

By then communism threatened, and Churchill once again issued warnings about a rising global threat. His weary nation voted him out of office not long after war's end, once again unable to endure his fiery warnings, but he was returned to office several years later, just as he was beginning to succumb to the strain of age. He lived the last decade of his life as one of the most honored men in history.

He had helped lead England through two world wars, a global depression, and the threat of communist subversion. His oratorical gifts had defined the great battles of his age and lifted the British people to their best. He also modeled a brand of leadership that will be emulated for generations. He was, indeed, the greatest man in the world at the end of his life.

This is but a brief outline of Churchill's life. I hope you will delve further into what he has to teach by reading his books as well as some of the brilliant volumes written about him. I've spent many hours at the great man's feet through the benefits of literature, and they have proven among the most transforming hours I've ever known.

I could not help but be moved by how much Churchill suffered. To know his story is to know that the inspiration he offered to the world in time of crisis was fashioned first in his own dark nights of the soul. He battled depression all his days. One of his children committed suicide, one died in infancy, and two let alcohol ruin their lives. Churchill made some disastrous decisions while in public office, and many in English society never forgave him. These comprise a small portion of the many hardships he endured.

The darkest specter that hovered over his life, though, was his father's near total disregard for him. It is hard to witness and even harder to explain, but it was one of the most defining forces in Churchill's life. What he became, both the flawed man and the heroic statesman, was fashioned largely by the crushing force of his father's hatred. We can pity Churchill for this agonizing experience, but we should also be grateful that in his battle to outstrip what could have been a deforming curse, he offers us vital lessons of true manhood.

It may help soften what we will be tempted to feel toward Winston's father to know he had contracted a disease that progressively affected his mind. Nearly all of Churchill's life, his father was slowly descending into madness. Knowing this might have helped a bit, but nothing can arm a boy against his own father's spite and derision.

Nearly from the time Winston was born, his father thought him retarded. He rarely spoke to his son, had little hope for his prospects, and wounded him often with his mounting rage. Winston's own son, Randolph, later wrote that "the neglect and lack of interest in him shown by his parents were remarkable, even judged by the standards of late Victorian and Edwardian days."[1] Randolph was speaking largely of his grandfather, who treated Winston with callous disregard.

As early as possible, Winston was shipped off to boarding school. His letters to his parents during this time rend the heart. He constantly pleaded for attention, spoke of how miserable he was, and begged for even a short visit from his parents. Nothing came of it. During this time it was not out of character for Lord Randolph to make a speech very near Winston's school, yet never cross the street to visit his son. He had determined, the troubled man once mysteriously said, to maintain before Winston "a stony and acid silence."[2]

What makes Lord Randolph's attitude toward Winston particularly difficult to stomach is how adoring and openhearted the boy was. Churchill himself later recounted how proud he had been when his father visited his room one day and took stock of Winston's vast collection of toy soldiers, all arrayed in battlefield formation. Randolph made a "formal visit of inspection" and "spent twenty minutes study-ing the scene—which was really impressive—with a keen eye and captivating smile. At the end he asked me if I would like to go into the Army. I thought it would be splendid to command an Army, so I said 'Yes' at once: and immediately I was taken at my word." The memory ought to have been a happy one for Winston, but the thrill left when he was eventually told of his father's motive: "For years I thought my father with his experience and flair had discerned in me the quali-ties of military genius. But I was told later that he had only come to the conclusion that I was not clever enough to go to the Bar."[3] Such wounds and disappointment haunted Churchill all of his life.

A more bruising episode occurred when a watch Winston's father had given him fell into a stream near a deep pool at Sandhurst. Though he was twenty years old at the time, Winston was terrified of his father's wrath. He instantly took off his clothes and plunged into the stream to look for the watch. Not finding it, he arranged to have the pool dredged. The watch still did not show itself. Winston decided to pay twenty-three soldiers to dig a new course for the stream and then he borrowed the school fire engine to pump the pool dry. Finally, he found the watch and sent it to a London watchmaker's shop for repair.

Somehow, his father learned what had happened. His angry letter reveals the blowtorch of derision Winston often faced. Lord Randolph assured his son that his conduct was "shameful," that he was a "young stupid" who was "not to be trusted," and that his younger brother, Jack, was "vastly" his "superior." It was an excessively harsh response to a fairly minor mistake. In later years, Winston would be able see his father's mental imbalance in this episode. At the time he had no filter, and the words lacerated his soul. Even when Churchill was nearing the end of his life, he sometimes thought he could hear his father's voice. Always it was scolding him for some misdeed. By then, Lord Randolph had been dead for half a century.

How did Churchill survive it? How did he overcome his father's bludgeoning to lead an exceptional life? He might easily have lived as a bitter, damaged man. He might have fulfilled one of his father's many curses—"you will become a mere social wastrel, one of the hundreds of public school failures, and you will degenerate into a shabby unhappy and futile existence"—and never served mankind as he did.[4] How did he keep his wounds from determining the course of his life?

The truth is that Churchill simply made a choice. He might have given himself to snarling bitterness and regret. Instead, he decided to see himself as an extension of the good in his father's life. He chose a pleasant continuity rather than a harsh antagonism.

We see this in his later account of his father's death in 1895. A lesser man might have rejoiced that the tyrant was dead. Winston wrote, "All my dreams of comradeship with him, of entering Parliament at his side and in his support were ended. There remained for me only to pursue his aims and vindicate his memory."[5] Clearly he had decided to let his father's vision propel him, to draw purpose rather than cancerous bitterness from his memories.

Winston also chose to weave this benevolent view of his harsh experience into a philosophy others could live by. Consider, for example, what these words have meant to those raised by fathers like Lord Randolph: "Solitary trees, if they grow at all, grow strong; and a boy deprived of a father's care often develops, if he escapes the perils of youth, an independence and vigour of thought which may restore in after life the heavy loss of early days."[6]

Consider also how many of Churchill's admirers must have taken comfort in this conclusion: "Famous men are usually the product of an unhappy childhood. The stern compression of circumstances, the twinges of adversity, the spur of slights and taunts in early years, are needed to evoke that ruthless fixity of purpose and tenacious mother wit without which great actions are seldom accomplished."[7]

Churchill managed to transform brutal treatment by a father into fuel for the great actions that marked his life. By doing so, he modeled a vital principle of manly living for us. This is to take nothing away from women, who sustain the same wounds men do—and often more of them. Yet women tend to handle pain and hardship better than most men do. They tend to be more realistic, less surprised by bruising experiences. This means they feel less personally betrayed by hurt and difficulty, so they are generally better able to let go of offense and move on in life. Men often seem perpetually stunned by the hard things that befall them. They can't seem to stop nursing their wounds and recounting their grievances. They pick at their scars and in the process make their wounds worse.

I'm sorry to be so blunt, gentlemen, but my experience is that, generally speaking, if a man does not arrive at a meaning for his pains— and if that meaning does not evolve into a mandate for his future—then he is very likely to allow his sufferings to crush him. He'll use them as an excuse for failure, a barrier against people, and a shield against his own emotions.

This is why Churchill's example is so important. His father brutalized him emotionally. Some scholars go so far as to say that Lord Randolph hated Winston. Yet Winston allowed these harsh winds to lift him to greater heights. Like a skilled glider pilot positioning himself to rise on thermal winds, Winston chose to position himself internally so that he ended up benefiting from his father's cruelty while he also lovingly extended his father's legacy. He never denied the pain and the torment of what he had been through, but he simply chose not to make them the epitaph over his life.

Thank God he did. Look at his impact upon the course of world history. Look at what might have been lost had he succumbed to the imprint of a mentally imbalanced man upon his life.

The good news for us is that Churchill did not outstrip his father's curses because he was an exceptional man. He became an exceptional man because he worked to outstrip his father's curses. We can do the same. It is not out of our reach. It is, instead, one of the skills of living out the full meaning of manhood.

WHAT THEN WILL YOU DO?
HOW WILL YOU SHOW YOURSELF A MAN?

1. Try to recall the most recent occasions when you have rehearsed the dark side of your past: the betrayals, the cruel words, the prophecies of doom, and the insults. Try to recall, also, the case you were making. Were you using your wounds to excuse yourself in some way? This case, supported by the evidence of your wounds, shows you the direction in which you are deforming your life through bitterness and self-pity. Look at it closely. It's your enemy.

2. Now consider your hardships and disappointments in Churchillian perspective. What did they mean for you that might be helpful? Did you hide in your room to escape a harsh parent, but then end up reading or practicing an instrument or lifting weights? Is there any good you can build upon from your otherwise painful experiences? And what good did the people who caused these pains leave for you? A coach might have humiliated you, but he may also have taught you how to work hard. A teacher may have insulted you for an entire school year, but she also may have spent ten minutes teaching something that changed your life. Search through the rubble. Find the good. Extend it.

3. Finally, act! Attempt "great actions." Stop excusing. Stop relieving yourself from duty. Do! Step out! Move forward! Achieve where you were supposed to fail. Make a difference where you were supposed to be inept. Answer the curses with a life well lived.

"BITTERNESS IS LIKE DRINKING POISON AND WAITING FOR THE OTHER PERSON TO DIE."

—*Joanna Weaver, from* Having a Mary Spirit: Allowing
God to Change Us from the Inside Out *(2006)*

ONLY A DAD

Only a dad, with a tired face,
Coming home from the daily race,
Bringing little of gold or fame,
To show how well he has played the game,
But glad in his heart that his own rejoice
To see him come, and to hear his voice.

Only a dad, with a brood of four,
One of ten million men or more.
Plodding along in the daily strife,
Bearing the whips and the scorns of life,
With never a whimper of pain or hate,
For the sake of those who at home await.

Only a dad, neither rich nor proud,
Merely one of the surging crowd
Toiling, striving from day to day,
Facing whatever may come his way,
Silent, whenever the harsh condemn,
And bearing it all for the love of them.

Only a dad, but he gives his all
To smooth the way for his children small,
Doing, with courage stern and grim,
The deeds that his father did for him.
This is the line that for him I pen,
Only a dad, but the best of men.

—EDGAR A. GUEST

FRIENDSHIP

THERE IS A PLAGUE THAT SOMETIMES WORRIES ME, AND IT IS not one of the great biological plagues we face today. I care about those, but the plague I think about almost every day is the plague of loneliness among men. In truth, the phrase that goes through my mind is this: *the friendless man.*

I talk to, consult with, counsel, and train a lot of men in the work I do. Most of these men are leaders, and some are known the world over. Almost every time I get a chance, I ask men about their friends. I learned a long time ago in my consulting work that friends are the best reflection of a man's happiness, priorities, and health.

What I usually hear from men is that they have simply lost touch with the men who mean the most to them. They find themselves awash in a sea of casual relationships. They do work with other men, and they can usually scare up a group of guys to go yell and scream at the sports bar. Yet when I ask them who they would turn to if they were about to have an affair or if their marriage was coming apart or if they were out of town and needed someone to get their son out of jail, most of them are at a loss to come up with a name. Some even tear up. Several guys I talked to were so lonely they asked me if I could recommend someone to be their friend.

The reasons for this plague would fill volumes. It would become a critical analysis of almost everything in the modern world. That's for another book. This book is about doing, about actions that make up manhood. I'm completely convinced that one of those actions—one of the skills we must master to be genuine men—is the skill of friendship.

If you snickered a bit when you read "skill of friendship," be assured I understand. For most men, friendships come easily. They certainly did for me. I never had to work at them. They didn't require a special set of skills to find buddies on the playground. In high school and college, finding friends was even easier.

Things changed after college, though. I got married. I bought a house. The grass around that house insisted on growing. I discovered that my wife came with all sorts of family members who, as it turned out, thought of me as a relative. This took time. Lots of it. I was also ambitious. I worked hard in my career and even decided to earn a couple of master's degrees. Then I lost my heart to two squirmy babies, and all of a sudden it was a decade and half later and I had started using the word *friend* to refer to guys in other cities whom I called once or twice a year. Maybe.

What I did not have was a band of brothers, a tribe, a posse, a group of guys who knew my life and were fun to be with but who had no problem challenging me if I needed it. You know: covenant, "one for all and all for one," and "always there for you, bro" kind of friends.

Fortunately, it wasn't long before I began to realize what had happened to me. This realization came because I heard someone say that by his early thirties the average man cannot name a friend close enough to even know what is going on in his life, much less to call up at the last minute for a bit of fun.

I was this average man. No other man knew what was happening in my inner life. No other man was close enough to see how I was living and even say an encouraging word, much less offer a warning if I needed it. And no wonderfully ill-mannered buddy was near enough to me to bust into my life and knock me out of my ruts and my routine. As a result, I was dull and getting duller. I was bored and boring. And I was stagnant, going absolutely nowhere but maintaining the illusion of progress. What I needed were other men to push me to my best and force me to come alive as a man. More simply, I needed friends.

Fortunately, I found some, and they kept me from the manhood-killing cancers of this life. I'm not exaggerating when I say these friends have made a massive difference in my life.

Hear me well, gentlemen: we will never become the men we are called to be unless we learn the art of friendship and intentionally cultivate deep, meaningful, rowdy relationships with other men.

This is one of the most important things for a man to know.

Of the men I have studied, my favorite example of covenant friendship is Jonathan, the son of King Saul of Israel. In my view, Jonathan lived a brand of friendship that not only changed the lives of his friends but changed nations as well. It's a high standard, but I think our friendships could have the same potential. Jonathan gives us a pattern for living out this potential.

He was a man of great spirit. I envision him as a bit of a wild man. Something about him seemed to draw boldness and nobility out of other men, and this is the key to understanding our first meaningful encounter with him in the pages of history.

We come upon Jonathan just as he is about to do something unorthodox, even insane. In the manner of big-hearted men of fiery spirit, he fully intends to talk another man into joining him in his insanity. This occurs when Israel is at war with its fiercest enemy, the Philistines. They are a people of the sea who seem unwilling to rest

until they destroy Israel entirely. There is intense hatred between the two peoples, but no one hates the Philistines like Jonathan. This is why, without telling his father, Jonathan has decided to attack a Philistine garrison. Alone.

Well, almost alone. He hopes to take his armor-bearer with him. It is important to picture this moment in your mind. Jonathan is crouched down behind rocks on a cliff high above a ravine. On the opposite side of this ravine is another cliff, and upon it is a Philistine camp. Jonathan watches it closely. Finally, he has seen enough and decides to make his move.

Now most men would be happy to leave these Philistines to another day. Most men would pace around and say something stupid like "Those Philistines had better be glad this ravine is between us or I'd make them pay."

Not Jonathan.

Instead, he turns to his armor bearer—who is probably no more than a burly teenager—and says, "Come, let's go over to the outpost of those uncircumcised men. Perhaps the LORD will act in our behalf. Nothing can hinder the LORD from saving, whether by many or by few" (1 Samuel 14:6 NIV).

I love that Jonathan makes no false promises. *Look,* he says, *the Lord can give us victory and he might. Or, he might not. Either way, let's go.*

His armor bearer responds to the magnetic spirit that permeates Jonathan's life: "Do all that you have in mind," he says. "I'm with you heart and soul" (v. 7).

Jonathan constantly elicits this kind of response from other men. He's all in. He makes others want to be all in too. We'll see what this means to a king and a nation in a moment.

It would make sense for Jonathan to lead his one armor bearer into the Philistine camp as quietly as possible. The whole plan is unwise, but the most he could hope for would be to do as much damage as possible before the Philistines rallied and began to overwhelm their attackers—all two of them. This, however, is not enough for Jonathan; not when the honor of Israel is at stake. Rather than remaining hidden, Jonathan decides to show himself to the Philistines. This, of course, is magnificently courageous and nuts. Why give away your position? Still, this is what Jonathan decides to do, and after he has done it, he decides to charge the Philistine camp.

It isn't easy. He and his aide climb down the face of their cliff, they cross the ravine, and then they climb up the face of the opposite cliff, all while the Philistines are yelling, "Come up to us and we'll teach you a lesson" (v. 12 NIV).

These taunts just make Jonathan more determined. So the two Israelites climb all the way up the face of the cliff. When they arrive at the top, the Lord is with them. They end up destroying the Philistine camp and killing twenty men.

You can imagine the bragging and celebrating in the Israelite camp later that night. It was Jonathan the troops would be celebrating. He was a man's man, and he kept making them all proud with his astonishingly heroic deeds. We can almost hear excited soldiers talking about what kind of king Jonathan is going to make.

This brings us to the friendship that changes a king, a nation, and the world.

Sometime later, on that day when a ruddy-faced shepherd boy has killed the Philistine giant called Goliath, Jonathan is standing nearby when Saul interviews the young champion, whose name is David. The king wants to know who David is and who his people are. While David tells his story, Jonathan is taken with the spirit of the man.

Listen to what the court historians wrote of this moment: "After David had finished talking with Saul, Jonathan became one in spirit with David, and he loved him as himself" (1 Samuel 18:1 NIV). Notice that Jonathan is drawn to the fire and the grit and the heart of David, to the spirit of God in his life, and loves him for these reasons first.

There is a lesson for us here. It is natural for our friendships to be largely about the things we do. We can have sports friends, work friends, and friends we make music with, for example. Yet covenant friendships have to be built on something more, on heart and purpose and matters of destiny. This convicted me when I first heard it. My friendships were usually thin and uninspiring. Perhaps yours are too. Thankfully, I started to realize that if I wanted friends who meshed with me at heart, with whom I could genuinely share life, I had to stop settling for friendships that were about little more than a few hours of fun and distraction. I had to do as Jonathan did—find men of spirit and devotion to God and build manly connections with them.

Jonathan isn't the kind of man to waste time. He sees David. He's drawn to his spirit. He loves him. He makes covenant with him. The record tells us: "Jonathan made a covenant with David because he loved him as himself. Jonathan took off the robe he was wearing and gave it to David, along with his tunic, and even his sword, his bow and his belt" (vv. 3–4 NIV).

Don't miss what is happening here. The son of the king has just about stripped to give covenant gifts to a shepherd boy. Why? Because he "became one in spirit with David, and he loved him as himself." So Jonathan initiated a friendship with covenant through sacrifice and heartfelt honor.

I imagine that two men like this do have a good deal of fun. They compete at everything from running to target practice. They probably also compete for the attention of women. They even compete for who can eat the most lamb. They laugh. They hit each other a lot. They are young champions enjoying a rowdy friendship.

Covenant is beneath it all, though, and this covenant is soon tested. David continues to be successful in battle and loved by the people.

This makes King Saul insanely jealous. He begins conspiring to kill David. Notice Jonathan. Though the king is his father, Jonathan does not side with him against his covenant friend. He knows this could cost him the throne. He knows his father's displeasure could ruin his future. Still, Jonathan has a covenant with David, and he will not break it, particularly when he knows Saul is committed to evil.

At the risk of everything that is rightfully his as the son of the king, Jonathan begins living out his costly commitment to David. First, he warns David of danger (see 1 Samuel 19:1–2). Every friendship, no matter how fun and rowdy it is, must be in part about guarding one another, about pointing out danger. Otherwise, it is no friendship. It is just two men using each other, unconcerned about each other's well-being.

Jonathan also courageously "spoke well" of David before his father (v. 4 NIV). This is risky. Saul is enraged. He's actually deranged. For Jonathan to defend David is sure to be seen by Saul as betrayal. Jonathan speaks up anyway. He's entered a covenant. And he sees what God is doing with his friend.

This, too, is part of covenant friendship. You don't betray with your words. You don't backstab. Correction happens in private. Gossip and undercutting never happen all. This is because all friendship is a form of covenant, a bond of mutual defense and support. And manly men keep their covenants.

This covenant of friendship keeps costing Jonathan dearly. He doesn't seem to mind. He loves his friend. He feels one with him in spirit. He knows he is meant to be part of God's work in David's life.

Soon, panic overtakes David. The constant pressure of Saul's enraged pursuit overwhelms him. To calm his friend, Jonathan meets him in secret and declares, "Whatever you want me to do, I'll do for you" (1 Samuel 20:4 NIV). In other words, *I'm yours. We're in covenant. How can I serve you? I'll do anything I can to help you.*

True friends serve each other. Love, history, and honor demand it.

You don't wring your hands when a friend is in need and hope someone else steps up. You go. You do what you can. You put yourself in the service of your covenant brother.

In fact, this covenant is so important to Jonathan that he renews it right in the middle of David's crisis (see vv. 16–17). Jonathan even expands the covenant, enlarging it from a covenant between two men to a covenant between dynasties: he covenants with the "house of David," the record tells us. The destiny of David's family line is in play and Jonathan pledges to support that line and defend it. Both men know what this means. Jonathan has just made a covenant to oppose his own father, even his father's house, in which Jonathan himself is the heir apparent.

While again defending David before Saul, Jonathan nearly loses his life. His father has become a man possessed and hurls a spear at his son in a delirious fit of rage (see v. 33). We should note quickly this costly truth: true friends stand in harm's way for each other. True friends take the hits for one another. It is cowardly to walk closely with a man to enjoy the benefits of his friendship but then abandon him when he is under attack. True friendships leave scars. Most men won't pay this price. It is why they will always live in a sea of casual relationships and discarded friends. Genuine men stand with their friends and look on the scars that result as signs of manly honor.

In time, David grows so tormented by Saul's conspiracies he barely realizes what Jonathan has done for him. Fear rules him. He's undone.

It would be a very good moment for Jonathan to leave the scene. His life is in danger, and his friend seems to be losing his mind. But Jonathan will not desert his friend or his covenant. When he realizes David is being pushed to the edge by all that is arrayed against him, Jonathan goes to David to help him "find strength in God" (1 Samuel 23:16 NIV).

This is a hallmark of manly friendship. True friends, covenant friends, instill faith and strength in each other. They make each other better over time than they were at the beginning. Yet if I am left dispirited and indifferent after I have been with my friends, then they are dumping their bilge into my life rather than helping me find my strength in God. We need more if we are going to be valiant, exemplary men. This doesn't mean there can't be fun. It doesn't mean every word we speak has to be from the King James Bible. We aren't fairies floating sweetly over a field of flowers. We're men! But the life of men together should make them better, not worse. It should not turn them from God or their wives or their duties. Instead, they should end up better, sharper, more rested, perhaps even smarter and wiser. Why not? Certainly, they should end up more eager to be genuine men.

Men help their friends find strength in God. It's part of the covenant.

Finally, there is an astonishing moment between Jonathan and David. Jonathan, who has long before understood what God is doing, declares to David, "You will be king over Israel, and I will be second to you. Even my father Saul knows this" (v. 17 NIV).

Remember, Jonathan is the son of the king of Israel, the rightful heir to the throne. He knows, though, what God intends to do with David, and he is completely devoted to it. He surrenders his right to the throne. He tells David what David probably already knows but isn't willing to say in front of the king's son: *David will be king.* And then Jonathan tenderly adds, "and I will be second to you."

I'm going to serve you, David. I'm going to have your back. I'm not going to flee the kingdom or lead a rebellion. I'll be right there as your number two.

In the manner of covenant men, the two renew their covenant once again. This is the third time they have sealed themselves to each other. It is what men in friendships do. They face life together, the good and the terrifying, the hilarious and the grievous. From time to time, they make covenant together at ever-deeper levels. This is because the friendship broadens and the challenges increase. The men change. They constantly rearticulate their manly devotion to one another with ever more heart-felt covenants. This is how true men bind themselves to their friends.

I wish I could tell you that Saul dies and David becomes king and he and Jonathan live many decades as friends while they lead Israel to glory. It would be a fine ending to the story. It just didn't happen that way. Instead, Saul and Jonathan are both killed in battle on the same day. David grieves his slain friend. Even years later he searches for some surviving member of Saul's house to whom he can be kind in Jonathan's memory.

It would be easy to see this as a story that does not end well. It isn't. The truth is that God used the covenant friendship between these two men not only to fill their lives with brotherhood and love but also to position one of them among the greatest kings in history. If Jonathan could speak to us now, we would not hear him bemoan his loss and his shortened life. We would hear him celebrate the greatness David achieved and the weighty friendship that played a role in God's great purposes.

How could we expect any less? Remember the kind of man Jonathan was: *Hey, armor bearer, I know you are only supposed to carry my armor so that I can do the fighting. But just in case God decides to do a miracle, let's scale up the face of this cliff with the enemy looking down, and let's wipe these fellows from the face of the earth. And let's do it after we've told them we're coming. Sound good to you?*

No, Jonathan wouldn't complain. He would just wish that he could have continued at David's side.

How do we live this out? This high and lofty friendship that shaped the course of history—is it beyond us? Is it more than men of our time can handle?

No. It is within the reach of every man. We devote ourselves to the principle that men cannot ascend to their best selves or their God-given purpose if they walk alone or if all they have in common with other men is entertainment or pleasure. Men need friends with whom they share a common spirit, a mutual devotion to each other's best, and a sacrificial commitment to protect, encourage, and defend. Men thrive only in vital, covenantal connection to other men—only if they are the spiritual sons of Jonathan, the willing friend of a shepherd named David.

Once all of this is established, of course, it is time for the manly rowdiness to begin!

WHAT THEN WILL YOU DO?
HOW WILL YOU SHOW YOURSELF A MAN?

1. Take stock of your friendships. Are they shallow, temporary, and unfulfilling? Do they lead you into something other than the paths of manly greatness? Or do they inspire you and make you yearn to be a great man, a manly man? Do you trust your friends, connect with them at a heart/spirit level, and rely on their wisdom and their example?

2. Is there a way to take the casual friendships you have now and deepen them so they look something like the friendship between Jonathan and David? How would the example of Jonathan give you wisdom for this?

3. What would it look like for you to make covenant with a close friend? What would it look like for you to help a friend find strength in God? In fact, take each of the meaningful moments between Jonathan and David described above, put them in your own words, and describe how you would live them out with your friends.

4. How might covenant friendships be abused and how can you guard against it?

5. How can you guide your wife and your children into covenant friendships?

6. Jonathan is described as a man of big heart and "great spirit." What does that mean? How would you become a man of great spirit? What would it mean for those in your life?

7. How can you help your generation of men escape the loneliness that haunts them?

"NO DISTANCE OF PLACE OR LAPSE OF TIME CAN LESSEN THE FRIENDSHIP OF THOSE WHO ARE THOROUGHLY PERSUADED OF EACH OTHER'S WORTH."

—*Robert Southey, from* The Doctor, *ed. John Wood Warter (1848)*

BLESSING

Gentlemen, I want to explore with you one of the great secrets of manhood, but I want to do it by way of repairing the reputation of one of the greatest men in American history. His name is General George S. Patton Jr.

Tell me. What flashed through your mind when you read that name? I understand completely if you thought of scenes from a movie rather than scenes from the man's life. This is exactly the reason Patton's reputation needs some repair!

In 1970, one of the most popular movies in Hollywood history opened in theaters. It was based on a script written in part by a young producer named Francis Ford Coppola. It featured eminent actor George C. Scott in a title role supported by a platoon of equally accomplished actors. It was magnificently filmed in Spain and Morocco and was stirringly accompanied by an award-winning musical score. It would earn huge ticket sales, win seven of the ten Academy Awards it was nominated for, and eventually be ranked among the top one hundred movies in history by numerous guilds and film historians.

This film was the epic *Patton*. There had simply been nothing like it before. From the opening scene in which George C. Scott's Patton makes a raw and inspiring speech—unannounced in any way by the film itself—to the closing scene in which Patton laments, "All glory is fleeting," the film proved itself the brilliant revelation of a man, a war, and American culture itself. Patton, already a revered figure, became the iconic fighting commander in the public's mind, and this occurred just as the war-torn 1960s limped wearily to an end.

As poignant and celebrated as the film was, it also tragically damaged the great general's reputation. There are dozens of inaccuracies and exaggerations in the script. Strangely, these distortions were likely intentional, the work of Patton's fellow officers in World War II.

When Patton had famously fallen out of favor and found himself without a command as war intensified in Europe, General Omar Bradley and General Dwight Eisenhower rescued him and gave him a lead role in the ultimate defeat of the Nazi regime. Patton knew what this had cost these friends and superior officers and was lastingly grateful. Unfortunately, after Patton died in 1946, his widow decided to release the general's private papers as a book entitled *War As I Knew It*. In its pages, Bradley and Eisenhower were scathingly criticized for being ineffective in command and weak in character. "Ike is more British than the British," Patton typically complained, "and is putty in their hands." Naturally, the two generals saw the deceased Patton as an ingrate and grew to resent him bitterly.

They may have sought their vengeance in the epic film of 1970. Both Eisenhower and Bradley served as advisors to the filmmakers, and it is possible their feelings of betrayal led to some of the inaccuracies depicted on the screen. Audiences left theaters believing that while Patton was a brilliant field commander, he was also obscene, insubordinate, blasphemous, casual with the lives of his soldiers, duplicitous, and something of a religious oddball who believed in reincarnation.

Little of this was true, yet the film's caricature embedded itself more deeply in the American psyche than did the facts of the great general's life. International audiences were urged toward this caricature even more aggressively. The British version of the film was titled *Patton–Lust for Glory*. This bitter revisionism has been a loss both to the nation and to the many men who might have benefited from Patton's example had it been more accurately depicted.

The real Patton was born in Los Angeles on November 11, 1885, a descendant of generations of American fighting men. It surprised no one when he entered Virginia Military Institute and then transferred to the United States Military Academy at West Point. His first years there were grueling. He was desperate to distinguish himself, though, and labored fiercely to overcome his deficiencies. He was rewarded in his final year when he achieved a high rank in his class, lettered in track and field, and even set a new school record in the 220-yard high hurdles. In his spare moments, he dreamed of reaching great heights. On the back of one of his textbooks, *Elements of Strategy*, Patton scribbled these lines:

"QUALITIES OF A GREAT GENERAL"

1. Tactically aggressive (loves a fight)
2. Strength of character
3. Steadiness of purpose
4. Acceptance of responsibility
5. Energy
6. Good health and strength

George Patton
Cadet
U. S. M. A.
April 29, 1909

Valiant dreams came naturally to him. They had been encouraged from childhood. His father first fueled his imagination by reading to him from Homer's *Iliad* and *Odyssey* and the novels of Sir Walter Scott. Young George was fed a steady diet of Shakespeare, as well. Visions of heroes and epic deeds were blended with religious faith in his early life, and this came through Bible reading, the lessons of *Pilgrim's Progress*, prayer, and his family's devotion to church. Though his coarse language and love of war drew more attention than his religious life in later years, Patton was a man who read the Bible daily, sought God on his knees, seldom failed to meet with his chaplains for prayer before a battle, and knew Scripture and Christian theology well enough to debate experts.

His early military career gave him reason to hope for greater glory. Distinction came rapidly. He competed as the army's representative in the pentathlon event of the 1912 Olympics, entered Mexico in search of Poncho Villa with General John "Blackjack" Pershing, and rose in rank largely because of his skills as a tank commander. He served heroically in France during the First World War, earning the Purple Heart and the Distinguished Service Medal. He returned home to acclaim as an armored warfare strategist and, despite the difficulties of American military life in the 1920s and 1930s, continued to rise in rank to become commander of the US Second Armored Division. This was the post he held on the eve of World War II.

We come, finally, to the moment in Patton's life that portrays a vital truth of genuine manhood. It occurred in the weeks just after the bombing of Pearl Harbor. The United States found itself suddenly at war with both Germany and Japan. Patton was given command of the Western Task Force with a single objective: drive German forces from North Africa. To achieve this Patton needed to defeat the legendary German tank commander Erwin Rommel and his Afrika Korps. He would lead the first great battle initiative to be undertaken by the United States Army in World War II.

He had dreamt of such a moment all of his life. These dreams sustained him through the arduous years of training, combat, and dreary duty at remote outposts. He was as prepared as his own effort and schooling by the army could make him.

Yet Patton knew he must have something more.

His mentor from his earliest days in the army had been the revered General John Pershing. Patton had been privileged to serve on Pershing's staff during World War I, had fought in Mexico under his command, and had continued to enjoy Pershing's favor in the years after. He had grown to love Pershing, a general who demanded steely discipline from his men yet routinely slept beside them on the ground and endured dangers at their side.

Patton had learned from Pershing's instructions and explanations, but he had also gained from the man's example. There was more to Pershing than skill and experience, even more than personality and character. Something invisible seemed involved in his sway over men, his strategic assessments, and his rule over himself. Patton concluded that the art of command is about more than what is seen. There are mystical qualities involved; empowerings that some men have and others do not. The art of command is about more than merely the sum of experience. As he prepared for a role in the greatest war mankind had ever known, Patton knew he would need this empowering, this grace, if he were to be a success.

This certainty led him to visit his old mentor at Walter Reed Army Medical Center just before leaving for Africa in 1942. Pershing had been ailing for some time and had become a permanent resident at the hospital. Patton greeted his former commander tenderly, moved once again by how profoundly the man had shaped his life. The two spoke of the war and of the state of the nation. When it was time for him to leave, Patton rose from his chair and said, "I came here to get your blessing, General." This moved Pershing, and he replied, "Kneel down,

Georgie." Patton knelt beside the old man's chair, allowing Pershing to lay his hand upon the younger warrior's head. He then said solemnly, "Goodbye, Georgie. God bless you, and keep you, and give you victory."[8]

When it was done, Patton rose, snapped to attention, and saluted his general. Pershing stood unsteadily and returned the salute. Patton left and later said he was thinking as he drove away from Walter Reed that he would never see General Pershing again. He was right.

The words of this blessing were few, and those looking on at the time surely thought them insignificant. Patton did not. He had come to respect the invisible realities of both life and command. He also understood how an older generation might have something supernatural to impart to the next. He wanted the empowering he had seen in Pershing's life. He believed—on the basis of his Bible reading, his Episcopal faith, and the history he knew so well—that such empowering might be transferred from one man to another, from the fathers to the sons. He wanted a hand placed upon him and the grace of God invoked by one who had known that grace in his own life. General George Patton would not think himself ready for his great task until that grace came also to him. He believed Pershing's blessing would make it so.

It is an important moment for us to observe, and we could not have understood it had the movie image of Patton been our only point of reference. The truth is that profane as Patton was, he was also a believer— in the existence of God, in the truth of Scripture, in the historic battle between good and evil, and in power given to men that they might fulfill their purpose. This was the reason he wanted the blessing of his military father before stepping onto the broader stage of his destiny.

Men are designed to live with a sense of connection to their ancestors. They want to feel they are living out a commission from their

fathers. Whether they realize it or not, they want to be sent into the future, to know importance in their lives that comes from heritage, tradition, and a generational purpose. In short, they want to belong to their ancestors in ways that liberate them and give their lives deeper meaning.

For centuries, men spoke of death as being "gathered to their fathers" (Judges 2:10 NIV). This created a sense of accountability to those who had come before them. Sons would think of themselves as carrying on the purposes of their fathers while also believing they would answer to their fathers at death. They didn't take this as bondage or an oppressive set of demands from the dead. Instead, they lived more gallant and useful lives inspired by the hopes that rested upon them.

For most men today, there is sadness in knowing this. I've felt it many times. Our broken families, generation gaps, and absentee or unengaged fathers leave men of my age longing for blessing and connection to the past but seldom knowing where to find it. We feel like generational orphans, like men without the fathers who might have laid one hand on us and another upon the past. We hunger for affirmation, impartation, and purpose. We want the blessing.

We should not despair. There is a God, and he can be a father to the fatherless. He can lead us into fields of honor while assuring the preparation, blessing, and ennobling purpose that others have had. The price may be, though—as with so much else that men of our generation lack—that God may meet us only after we have gone in pursuit.

We should not hesitate to go after this connection to heritage and find it where we can. I have friends who never knew their fathers yet who knelt before elderly veterans to ask their blessing. My friends later said they simply wanted someone who had lived a noble life to ask that God's grace might be upon them. I know other men who studied their family and ethnic history and crafted their own liturgies in which they asked God together to grant them the spirit of their righteous ancestors. I have one friend who searched for years to find even a distant male relative who might bless him and stand with him in asking God to restore their lost family purpose. All these men were dramatically changed once they stopped lamenting what they did not have and went in pursuit of the best they could have.

We should not think of ourselves as men without heritage or belonging. We have fathers—of faith, of our national life, in our ethnic heritage, and even among extended family. We should work to restore the links to an elevating past wherever we can find them.

Let me briefly tell you how this unfolded in my life. As I've explained, my father was a good soldier and a heroic American, but he kept an emotional distance from his sons. Having lived with this for my first eighteen years, I expected little more when I left home to build a family of my own. I had made my peace with it. It helped that I had become a Christian and had spiritual fathers and older friends who seemed to fill the void.

All was well until a series of experiences—reading about Patton kneeling before Pershing was one of them—made me yearn for anything I could carry forward as a son from my father's life. I knew better than to do as some of my friends had done and ask my father to put his hands on me and speak an invocation. It would have been met with sarcasm and dismissal. It would have embarrassed him. I didn't want to give opportunity for further damage.

I decided to turn the process around. Rather than ask my father to bless me—something he would not have understood or known how to do—I decided to bless him. I wrote a long letter to him thanking him for all the good that had come to me through his life. I wrote about the places I had lived because of his career and how these experiences had changed me. I described the benefits of military culture for an American boy growing up in the 1970s. I described how living in Berlin, Germany, during the Cold War had set me apart from my friends and given me a love of country and freedom I would never have otherwise known.

I also wrote all I could about his character. He had been a good soldier, had come home at six o'clock every evening for dinner when he was not at war, had been generous with his children, and had given us lovely, ordered homes. It never crossed my mind a father might enter his son's room at night for any vile purpose. It never crossed my mind that the few bottles of alcohol in our home could mean destruction or that my mother might be secretly suffering violence. These possibilities never entered my mind because they weren't happening in our family—a tribute, in part, to this decent, dutiful, even heroic man.

The letter I received in return was the closest my father could come to a blessing. He spoke, in military terms, of pride in my performance and certainty that I would continue to rise. Yet he also said that he had spent several hours in tears before writing me and that he was touched by my letter as he had seldom been in his life. I knew we had made a connection and that the man had simply given as much as he had to give.

It was enough. I could carry my father's hopes and expectations, the more honorable elements of his example, and, certainly, his exemplary service to his country, forward. This, combined with the men God has put around me and the heritage of heroic faith I have by virtue of simply being a Christian, is enough commission and heritage to fill my soul.

Some men have magnificent fathers who give their sons all a father should. Some men have no fathers at all. Others have fathers so unengaged they might as well not exist. Some men have fathers who by their conduct have made enemies of their families.

True manhood faces each of these difficult conditions bravely, determined to heal and rise above. And true men then draw from the wells of heritage, generational purpose, and legacy that are available to them in order to live out noble, honorable lives. It isn't easy, yet it can be done. There is a blessing to be had.

WHAT THEN WILL YOU DO?
HOW WILL YOU SHOW YOURSELF A MAN?

1. Make sure you are certain about the meaning of the word *blessing*. Look up the various forms of the word in the Bible and write down the verses that pertain to an older man or woman blessing a child or someone of the next generation. Scan for the concept in history, your ethnic or tribal history in particular. You might also read some of the better books that explore this concept from a biblical perspective.

2. Who is in a position to bless you? Your father, your tribal leader, the older males in your family, your spiritual mentors, or perhaps other relatives—all are possibilities. Keep in mind that mothers and other women in your life are candidates as well.

3. If a blessing is a passing on of the good in past generations, investigate the good elements of your family line, your tribe, your people. What is it you would like for a blessing to draw out of your people's past?

4. Along with other men who form your "band of brothers," craft a blessing ritual or ceremony. If your church already has a ritual of this kind, meet with your clergyman to see how it applies to your life. These rituals or ceremonies need not be highly complex, but should include a season of preparation, both extemporaneous and written declarations of blessing, witnesses, people designated to lay on hands and speak the blessing, and, finally, some type of commemorative object (a sword, a mug, grandfather's tie clasp, dad's army swagger stick, a kilt, a book, and so forth).

"IF THE YOUNG ARE NOT INITIATED INTO THE VILLAGE, THEY WILL BURN IT DOWN JUST TO FEEL ITS WARMTH."

—African proverb

A NATION'S STRENGTH

What makes a nation's pillars high
And its foundations strong?
What makes it mighty to defy
The foes that round it throng?

It is not gold. Its kingdoms grand
Go down in battle shock;
Its shafts are laid on sinking sand,
Not on abiding rock.

Is it the sword? Ask the red dust
Of empires passed away;
The blood has turned their stones to rust,
Their glory to decay.

And is it pride? Ah, that bright crown
Has seemed to nations sweet;
But God has struck its luster down
In ashes at his feet.

Not gold but only men can make
A people great and strong;
Men who for truth and honor's sake
Stand fast and suffer long.

Brave men who work while others sleep,
Who dare while others fly . . .
They build a nation's pillars deep
And lift them to the sky.

—RALPH WALDO EMERSON

QUEST

IF YOU ARE A HUNTER, YOU MAY ALREADY KNOW WHY SOME OF our founding fathers wanted the national symbol to be the turkey rather than the eagle. As beautiful as they are, eagles are scavengers. The founding fathers were men still taming a wilderness, and they knew this. They weren't impressed. They were impressed with the turkey. If you have ever hunted turkeys, you were probably impressed too.

They are unbelievably fast creatures, capable of running twenty-five miles per hour and flying at speeds up to fifty-five miles per hour. They are also smart and constantly on the alert. Hunters like to say a deer thinks every hunter is a tree stump but a turkey thinks every tree stump is a hunter. They can be hard to find, harder to kill, and then, just to be ornery, turkeys make themselves hard to clean after they're dead. There are as many as fifty-five hundred feathers on an adult turkey.

This is the wild turkey, though. The domesticated turkey is another story. They are idiots, perhaps the dumbest animals alive. Domesticated turkeys will eat themselves to death unless someone stops them. If thunder frightens them, they will often bunch up in one corner of their pen and suffocate each other.

Interesting, isn't it? In the wild, turkeys are amazing. When domesticated, turkeys are so stupid they have to be kept from accidentally killing themselves a dozen different ways.

Gentlemen, let's admit it: most of us are tragically overdomesticated. We have hardly any connection to the wild or our wilder selves. Words like *adventure, exploit,* and *quest* no longer apply to us. It is why we are soft, whiney, and bored.

Let's let the words of some wise ones convict us.

Men of age object too much, consult too long, adventure too little, repent too soon, and seldom drive business home to the full period, but content themselves with a mediocrity of success.

—Francis Bacon, "Of Youth and Age, "from
The Essays; Or Counsels, Civil and Moral

I think that sense of adventure gets tamed out of us. We also get frightened. Somewhere along the way, a man loses that confidence, that recklessness or fearlessness he had as a boy. Somewhere along the story of his life, doubt comes in. And a doubt goes like this: "No you don't. You don't have what it takes. You can't come through. You can't pull this off. So just put your nose to the horse in front of you and get in line and just become a gelding. Tie your reins up there at the corporate corral and give up any sense of risk."

—John Eldredge, in *10 Passions of a Man's Soul* (2006)

Security is mostly a superstition. It does not exist in nature, nor do the children of men as a whole experience it. Avoiding danger is no safer in the long run than outright exposure. Life is either a daring adventure, or nothing.

—Helen Keller, from *The Open Door* (1957)

I read these words, and I know I've lost something. I've become a domesticated turkey. God help me. I've had the risk and the daring and the need for adventure squeezed out of me by duty and the ease of modern life. I don't plan to stay this way.

My inner GPS needs resetting if I'm going to navigate the geography of manliness. Perhaps taking a good look at a man who mapped that geography more than a century ago will help me recover myself. Come along with me.

Let's consider the life of Jedediah Smith, one of the greatest explorers and mountain men in American history. His list of firsts is stunning. He was the first white man to journey overland to the Great Salt Lake, the Colorado River, and the Mojave Desert. He was the first US citizen to explore the Sierra Nevada and the Great Basin in an eastward direction. He was the first American to journey through California to the Oregon Country. He also discovered the famous South Pass that pioneers used in droves to reach the Oregon region. His discoveries and explorations changed the westward expansion of the nation and thus the nation itself. In the process, he survived three massacres, some of the coldest weather on record, and mauling by a bear.

These achievements would be magnificent had he lived a hundred years, but he died at the age of thirty-two, having begun his journeys only a decade before.

Smith was born in Jericho, New York, on January 6, 1799. He came from two God-fearing New England families and had the good fortune to be mentored by a series of godly men. In his early years, two Methodist circuit riders taught him much of what they knew. Later, Dr. Titus G. V. Simons, a pioneer physician close to the Smith family, instilled in young "Diah" a love of nature and adventure. Simons gave

his young friend a copy of Lewis and Clark's 1814 chronicle of their epic journey to the Pacific Ocean. Smith read the classic, acquired a hunger for adventure from its pages, and kept it at his side for the rest of his life.

In 1822, twenty-three-year-old Smith stumbled upon an advertisement that changed his life. It was General William Ashley's famous call for adventurous men.

TO

Enterprising Young Men

The subscriber wishes to engage ONE HUNDRED MEN, to ascend the river Missouri to its source, there to be employed for one, two or three years.—For particulars enquire of Major Andrew Henry, near the Lead Mines, in the County of Washington, (who will ascend with and command the party) or to the subscriber at St. Louis.

Wm. H. Ashley

The men who responded to this call became known as "Ashley's Hundred." Smith was one of them. He made several trips with Ashley up and down the Missouri River, often retracing the route Lewis and Clark had taken. Hardship and deadly skirmishes with natives tested him, but Smith knew he had discovered his life's work. A year later, barely twenty-four years old, he was made captain of one of Ashley's boat crews. His first assignment was to explore uncharted portions of the territory that would eventually become Montana.

Smith made many such trips during his short life. His great courage and yearning to see uncharted lands, along with the fearful difficulties he encountered, made him a legend even among legendary men.

For decades after he died, for example, men sat around campfires and told of the time he was stalked and attacked by a massive grizzly. The great beast tackled him, gashed open his side and took his head entirely in its jaws. Smith fought valiantly until the animal retreated at the sudden sound of approaching men. He was so mangled his men thought he was dead. His scalp had been torn jaggedly open, and his ear had been ripped from the side of his head. After his wounds were washed, Smith calmly instructed one of men in the proper method for sewing on his ear and closing his scalp. The scars this left added to the legend of the man, as did the long hair he grew to cover over his wounds.

On another occasion, as Smith led a party over the western mountains, winds blew so furiously that the side of one mountain was blown completely clean of snow, and the buffalo who usually grazed nearby stampeded to safer ground. Each night of this ordeal the men stayed awake to keep their blankets and heavy coats from blowing away. When they finally were able to light a fire, the wind blew the logs off the mountain. They endured these conditions for two days.

Realizing they had to descend, the party followed a creek downward into a canyon. There they huddled together for warmth. Frigid hours passed before they looked up at a ridge above them and saw a mountain sheep. The wind was still blowing so powerfully that, as the men watched from below, the animal was swept off of its ridge and slid down the face of a cliff before coming to a stop just at the feet of the hungry men. The stunned sheep was an easy kill. In *Jedediah Smith and the Opening of the American West*, Dale L. Morgan concluded his description of this episode with these words: "Clyman [one of Smith's men] rose shivering from his blankets, made a fire and began to broil thin slices of meat. The savory odor aroused his companions, and the rest of the night they cooked, ate and told one another lies."[9]

Such is the way of men. More important than these adventures to Smith was the power of his faith. He was descended from Massachusetts ancestors who knew and admired the Pilgrims of Plymouth. His people were fiercely Christian and bold. One of them, a pious man, was among the first to go over Niagara Falls and live to talk about it. Jedediah was of the same spirit. His men knew he always carried a Bible in his shirt pocket. They knew, also, that while they attacked a freshly cooked meal, Smith would first raise his voice in thanksgiving to God, which was both a genuine expression of gratitude and a rebuke to his crew for their pagan manners. He had memorized many lengthy passages of Scripture on his long, often solitary journeys and he routinely quoted verses aloud for miles on end as he traveled. His men may not have shared his faith, but they took comfort in their captain's connection to God.

Jedediah Smith was an extraordinary man, but more important for us is that he was a man fully alive, devoted to adventure, and ever in search of the new and unexplored.

I'm being very open with you in this chapter. The Jedediah Smith part of me is in danger of dying early, just like the actual man. I have a pretty fantastic life. I travel. I speak. I work with powerful people. I appear on television. I have the wife of my dreams and children I love from the heart.

Is it enough? Yes, but this is not all there is to a man. Let's be blunt. Men need to bark at the moon. Men need to blow something up. Men need to push themselves into a zone they don't control—that in fact isn't actually a zone.

Men need to go in pursuit. They need a quest.

This doesn't happen much in my life. But it is going to. And you? Can you afford to lose this massive part of who you really are? I don't think so. Nor do I think any of the men in our generation can afford to see this adventure-seeking part of themselves as dispensable.

I'm going to give the last word on this to a man I admire, who knows a thing or two about adventure. He's Jon Krakauer, the author of *Into the Wild, Into Thin Air, Under the Banner of Heaven,* and *Where Men Win Glory.* Listen:

> Make a radical change in your lifestyle and begin to boldly do things which you may previously never have thought of doing, or been too hesitant to attempt. So many people live within unhappy circumstances and yet will not take the initiative to change their situation because they are conditioned to a life of security, conformity, and conservation, all of which may appear to give one peace of mind, but in reality nothing is more damaging to the adventurous spirit within a man than a secure future. The very basic core of a man's living spirit is his passion for adventure. The joy of life comes from our encounters with new experiences, and hence there is no greater joy than to have an endlessly changing horizon, for each day to have a new and different sun. If you want to get more out of life, you must lose your inclination for monotonous security and adopt a helter-skelter style of life that will at first appear to you to be crazy. But once you become accustomed to such a life you will see its full meaning and its incredible beauty.[10]

I don't know what Jon Krakauer believes about spiritual things. I do know he believes the right things about a man's need for adventure. I also know that God made me, he made me to live a fully engaged life; and to press against some frontier, push myself beyond my ease, and let my soul feel itself under threat. My first-class airplane seat, Hilton Hotel room, steak at Morton's, iPad-addicted, way-overlauded life is not helping me be this kind of man.

Stay tuned. I'll be back.

WHAT THEN WILL YOU DO?
HOW WILL YOU SHOW YOURSELF A MAN?

1. Get and read John Eldredge's *Wild at Heart*. It's the best book on this subject.
2. Remember the last time your heart raced, you sweated like a pig, you thought you might die, you conquered something, and you bored your band of brothers to death by describing it over and over again? Go do something like it again. Just don't get arrested.
3. Then train for something bigger.
4. Finally, find me and make sure I'm doing the same.

> ## "WITHOUT ADVENTURE CIVILIZATION IS IN FULL DECAY."
> —*Alfred North Whitehead, from* Adventures of Ideas *(1933)*

LIFE'S MIRROR

There are loyal hearts, there are spirits brave,
There are souls that are pure and true;
Then give to the world the best that you have,
And the best will come back to you.
Give love, and love to your life will flow,
A strength in your utmost need;
Have faith, and a score of hearts will show
Their faith in your work and deed.
Give truth, and your gift will be paid in kind,
And honor will honor meet;
And the smile which is sweet will surely find
A smile that is just as sweet.
Give sorrow and pity to those who mourn;
You will gather in flowers again
The scattered seeds from your thought outborne
Though the sowing seemed but vain.
For life is the mirror of king and slave,
'Tis just what we are and do;
Then give to the world the best that you have
And the best will come back to you.

—MADELINE S. BRIDGES

HUMOR

The English essayist William Hazlitt wrote in *Lectures on the English Comic Writers* (1819), "Man is the only animal that laughs and weeps: for he is the only animal that is struck by the difference between what things are and what they ought to be." I think these words beautifully capture how men use humor, and they remind me of one of my favorite "great man" stories, a story that illustrates man humor at a critical moment in history.

It comes, as do so many other wonderful stories, from the life of Winston Churchill. During the years when England's political left was systematically nationalizing the nation's industries and services, Churchill walked out of a raucous session of Parliament to use the men's room. This was in the days when the urinal was often a long metal or porcelain trough running the length of the room. While Churchill was relieving himself, one of the leading nationalizers entered the room and began doing his business right next to Churchill. The irritated conservative moved to the far end of the trough. "Feeling a bit stand off-ish today, Winston?" the new arrival asked mockingly.

"No," growled Churchill. "But whenever you see anything big, you want to nationalize it."

Now this, gentlemen, is perfect. It is a lesson in the art of manly humor. First, it is funny enough that you can't wait to retell it. That's important. Man humor has to have a sufficient laugh factor to qualify it for going viral. Second, it makes a point. In fact, it makes a very good point. *Here, let me hide my privates so that your mindless socialism doesn't mistake it for something the nation should own.* Third, it draws blood. Man humor doesn't always have to be the verbal equivalent of taking a swing at another man. Sometimes man humor is encouraging, or just entertaining and distracting. But when humor is needed to make an enemy feel pain, Churchill's example is the way to go. Finally, it is slightly crude. Men like this. For a man to score a philosophical point by referring to a body part in such a way that his opponent can't help but laugh too—now that is a Manly Moment of Victory.

Manly humor accomplishes many tasks, but most often it is like the ping of a submarine's radar. *Is there anyone out there? Am I safe being a true man with you?*

Manly humor also explores the nature of things. Women reading this book might turn to their husbands and say, "Winston Churchill was *crude!*" But men know that Churchill was stating a broad truth about an important matter. *You liberals are nationalizing everything you can in our society. But, listen up: it isn't yours! It shouldn't be nationalized just because it is big! And you're probably just envious anyway!*

Finally, in more serious situations, man humor confronts fear and prepares the heart for action. It's a tool for dealing with danger, quieting panic, and calling comrades to prepare to charge. Call it gallows humor. Call it foxhole humor. Wherever it happens, it is how men use the sometimes crass but always funny comment to force a laugh and encourage their brothers-in-arms. *Well, here we are, facing these monsters. At least we're all together. And these idiots probably aren't as fierce as we've been told. I hear they can't find their manhood with a flashlight. Let's take these fools!*

Manly humor is one of the great joys of being a man. It is also one of the tools in the tool set of truly great men.

Comparable to Churchill in his use of humor was the English writer G. K. Chesterton, whose comedic style exhibited the kind of wonder and joy that arises from a Christian worldview. Though Chesterton is best known for his Father Brown detective novels, his biography of St. Thomas Aquinas, and his classic apologetic work *Orthodoxy*, he wrote much more, including eighty books, two hundred short stories, and four thousand articles. His writing was profoundly influential. Men as esteemed as Mahatma Gandhi, Bishop Fulton Sheen, and the Irish Republican leader Michael Collins acknowledged his influence upon them. Chesterton's *The Everlasting Man* even played a critical role in C. S. Lewis's conversion. He was certainly one of the great minds of the twentieth century.

Yet he was also, unquestionably, an oddball. He was physically gigantic—roughly six-foot-four and three hundred pounds—with a great mop of unkempt hair. He liked to joke that he had to be the most polite man in England because when he gave up his seat on a bus it meant that four women could sit in his place. He made a striking impression in his cape, crumpled hat, and walking stick, and seldom allowed much time to pass between cigars. He was also clumsy and astonishingly absentminded. He routinely sent telegrams to his wife to get help in finding his way. "Am at Aldersgate. Where am I supposed to be?" he would write. "Home," she would often reply.

It may be that this disorientation to the real world was the price

of his keen mind and sense of wonder. Chesterton saw the universe as filled with benevolent mystery. He believed a loving God designed creation to appeal to the curiosity and intellectual hunger of mankind. It is the reason he wrote articles about such seemingly trivial matters as chalk, lying in bed, and "what I found in my pocket."

It is also the basis for his humor. When the younger sister of his fiancé was tragically killed, Chesterton insisted upon writing his love long letters of "rambling levity" during the worst of her grief. He told a friend, "I have sworn that Gertrude should not feel, wherever she is, that the comedy has gone out of our theater."

He believed that no work of God should be untouched by levity, even death. When giving instructions to his wife about his funeral, he wrote, "If there occurs to anyone a really good joke about the look of my coffin, I command him by all the thunders to make it. If he doesn't I'll kick the lid up and make it myself . . . No, darling, if we are picking flowers we will not hide them if a hearse goes by."[11]

His sense of wonder gave him a love of children, and he fabricated great schemes to involve them and enflame their imaginations. He once organized the Society for the Encouragement of Rain, which in England was not unlike creating an organization devoted to the preservation of snow in Alaska. Chesterton made membership cards and named his wife's niece as President Rhoda Bastable and himself Secretary G. K. Chesterton. The bylaws of the organization required meetings to be held "on the Salisbury Plain where under the sign of an umbrella members were invited to partake of cakes and coffee in the rain."[12]

Keep in mind that this man we see creating a fictional society with children was described by one scholar as "one of the deepest thinkers who ever existed."[13] A pope called him a gifted defender of the faith. Even one of his greatest opponents said that the world is not thankful enough for him. And his biographer, Dale Alquist, argued, "G. K. Chesterton was the best writer of the twentieth century. He said something about everything, and he said it better than anybody else."[14] Yet Chesterton dreamed of coffee on the Salisbury Plain with children—in the rain—and could not go to the store for milk without forgetting where he was meant to be because he was pondering the meaning of pocket lint.

He was a man of humor, fun, and fascination with the wonder of the universe and a great hunger to know. It made him exceptional, one of the giants of his age. Consider these witticisms, culled from his volumes of writing:[15]

"Art, like morality, consists of drawing the line somewhere."

"By experts in poverty I do not mean sociologists, but poor men."

"Once I planned to write a book of poems entirely about the things in my pocket. But I found it would be too long; and the age of the great epics is past."

"Do not free the camel of the burden of his hump; you may be freeing him from being a camel."

"Fallacies do not cease to be fallacies because they become fashions."

"I believe in getting into hot water. I think it keeps you clean."

"I've searched all the parks in all the cities and found no statues of committees."

"Journalism consists largely in saying 'Lord James is dead' to people who never knew Lord James was alive."

"Merely having an open mind is nothing; the object of opening the mind, as of opening the mouth, is to shut it again on something solid."

"Moderate strength is shown in violence, supreme strength is shown in levity."

"No man knows he is young while he is young."

"One of the great disadvantages of hurry is that it takes such a long time."

"People generally quarrel because they cannot argue."

"The Christian ideal has not been tried and found wanting. It has been found difficult and left untried."

"There is no man really clever who has not found that he is stupid."

"The poor have sometimes objected to being governed badly; the rich have always objected to being governed at all."

"The reformer is always right about what is wrong. He is generally wrong about what is right."

"To be clever enough to get all the money, one must be stupid enough to want it."

Laughing, joking, teasing, and storytelling are some of the best experiences in life. They enrich our days, bind us to others, teach us, and make life sweet and endurable. They are gifts from God and fruits of humility and wonder, since they are only possible when we see the flaws of the world but content ourselves with the knowledge that even flaws have purpose in the plan of God. We can relax then and laugh, crack the joke, or tell the funny story because we know our seriousness changes nothing. God rules, and we are free to delight in this fact and use humor to endure the way things are while we await the perfection that is coming.

Genuine men understand the power and meaning of humor. Some have greater gifts for joking and storytelling than others, but all can at least understand why humor is important, what it does for the soul of the fearful and hurting, and why it is so essential to what a man is made to do. Humor allows us to lighten the heart, encourage our children when they fail, ease stress from our wives, motivate younger men, and unify friends. Humor also allows us to drain the terror from our souls before battle.

It can also be a tool for seizing the moment for a greater good. No one was more skilled at this than Winston Churchill, and it would be fitting to end this chapter with a few of his more brilliant performances.

In the darkest days of World War II, Churchill lived with the Roosevelts at the White House during the many days required to determine strategies and negotiate matters like US aid for England. Many Americans in Congress and in the press charged that Churchill was being deceptive by asking for far more aid than England needed. Suspicions swirled in newspaper headlines. Tensions were thick even as Roosevelt and Churchill met.

One day Churchill emerged from his bath—he bathed every day, sometimes several times a day—just as an aide wheeled Roosevelt into Churchill's room. Seeing the prime minister of England wrapped in a towel, the embarrassed Roosevelt ordered his aide to wheel him out so Churchill could have his privacy. Astutely, Churchill seized the moment for a larger cause. Holding up a detaining hand, he removed the towel and solemnly proclaimed, "The prime minister of Great Britain has nothing to hide from the president of the United States." Churchill's point was made, and history was changed because of it.

Finally, there were several women who irritated Churchill. Unfortunately, he found himself at dinners with each of them. One was Lady Astor, ever a thorn in his side. During their conversation one evening, Lady Astor grew so exasperated with Churchill that she exclaimed, "Winston, if I were your wife I'd poison your soup." He replied without hesitation, "Nancy, if I were your husband, I'd drink it." On another occasion, the second woman who bedeviled Churchill informed him that she liked neither his politics nor the new mustache he was sporting. He retorted, "Madam, I see no earthly reason why you should come into contact with either."

Churchill wrote, "In my belief, you cannot deal with the most serious things in the world unless you also understand the most amusing."[16] He, like Chesterton, teaches us that humor is more than a form of play. It grows from our view of the world. It is a tool of manly leadership. It is a gracious gift from God as we live in a troubling world. Thank God for Chesterton and Churchill!

WHAT THEN WILL YOU DO?
HOW WILL YOU SHOW YOURSELF A MAN?

1. Take stock of your own sense of humor for a moment. Have you put this valuable gift in the service of anger, bitterness, and hate? Do you use humor only to wound and control? If so, clean it up. Repent before God, apologize to those you've damaged, and begin putting your gift for humor in the service of nobler ends.

2. Practice good humor. Yes. That's exactly what I mean. Even the dullest man can learn a few jokes and tell them to wring a laugh when needed. If you've told dirty jokes and stories all your life, start learning new ones. Get a book. Go on a clean joke website. Watch a clean comedian. Also, if you have a hard time telling a joke with any sense of timing, get some help. Find someone who can work with you a bit. Here is the heart of the matter: If humor is as powerful a tool as I've said it is in this chapter, then it is worth practicing to get right. It is also worth falling flat for a while. Anything worth doing is worth doing badly until you do it well.

3. Start using humor at moments when it will help. The dinner conversation turns sour. Your daughter is discouraged. Your son didn't make the team or get the girl. The staff needs to lighten up after a slow season of sales. Obviously, I don't mean to make light of suffering, but having offered the usual comfort, lighten the mood. The man I know who does this best is the worst joke teller in the world. His kids moan as soon as he starts. He knows how bad he is. In truth, his joke is

that he's trying to tell a joke. I've noticed, though, that when he starts up and his kids moan and tell him to stop, they are already laughing. The victory is already his. He's loving his children in the language of humor. He's healing their wounds and telling them life is full of diasppointments but it is still sweet and good. Mission accomplished.

4. Finally, learn a lesson from Joel Osteen, whether he's your kind of minister or not. Joel can't tell a joke to save his life. People obviously collect jokes for him. Yet at the beginning of every sermon he says, "I always like to start out with something funny" and then he tells a joke. It is one joke, announced flatly and often told badly. Yet it works. Why? Because making humor a priority, even if less than skillfully accomplished, is a victory of its own. People love Joel for trying, though they would never repeat some of his truly horrible jokes. Joel isn't trying to be a comedian, though. He's trying to draw people in and make a connection with them. It works. Now, when the pastor's joke gets crowded out of a service, people write to Joel to tell him how they missed it, how it somehow made their week a bit less than usual. Remember, this is one joke, announced flatly, and often told badly. That's the power of humor.

> ### "HUMOR IS THE PRELUDE TO FAITH AND LAUGHTER IS THE BEGINNING OF PRAYER."
> —*Reinhold Niebuhr, from* Discerning the Signs of the Times: Sermons for Today and Tomorrow *(1949)*

RESTORATION

My father rarely spoke about what he felt or believed. He was an army officer, which made him demanding about performance but almost entirely uninterested in why anyone performed. His message, even to his sons, was "believe what you want but perform as I tell you."

In fact, he once said to me—probably to tweak my mother who was a devoted Christian—"I'll tell you what you can believe. You can believe that if the yard isn't mowed by three this afternoon, judgment day will descend. The last trumpet will sound for you!"

That was Dad.

I was surprised, then, when he offered a little insight into his soul between football games on a Saturday afternoon in 1977. I was home from college for the Christmas holidays and was "spending time" with Dad, which meant watching football from mid-morning to midnight.

When the second game of the day ended, and we were reprovisioning for the third, Dad rubbed his hands together eagerly, said something about how pitifully a certain quarterback had been playing, and then declared to the television in our kitchen, "But maybe it will be different today. I love to see a man improve upon himself."

This may seem insignificant, but it was one of only four or five insights into Dad's soul I was ever allowed. Like the others, this one came to me almost by accident. Dad wasn't even talking to me when he said it. He was talking to his "best friend," the anchor of CBS Sports.

I've never forgotten it and, in a way I can't fully explain, Dad's words left me with a fascination for people who fail and then strive to overcome it. I've studied them in history. I've tracked them in the headlines. In time, I even gained a reputation for counseling men who had known disaster but who were determined to rise again. Some of them rebuilt. Some did not. As each story unfolded, I thought of my father and his words: "I love to see a man improve upon himself."

Through all of this, I began to understand that the simple willingness to fight back after misfortune is one of the most important features of genuine manliness. Women certainly face these crises, too, but frankly they seem to me more courageous and capable at such moments. Men seem more likely to doubt themselves, more likely to put a bullet through their heads or live the rest of their lives at the bottom of a bottle. The statistics bear this out. Losing all and reclaiming it again while friends keep a suspicious distance and the words of critics sear the soul—these seem to me about the hardest things a man can face, and it is not surprising that many men never recover themselves.

Rudyard Kipling said it well in his poem "If—," in which he almost perfectly defined the manly virtues for all time. The stanzas about a man losing all and rebuilding again have always seemed to me a fleshing out of my father's single sentence.

If you can bear to hear the truth you've spoken
Twisted by knaves to make a trap for fools,
Or watch the things you gave your life to, broken,
And stoop and build 'em up with worn-out tools:

If you can make one heap of all your winnings
And risk it on one turn of pitch-and-toss,
And lose, and start again at your beginnings
And never breathe a word about your loss . . .
You'll be a Man, my son!

Now there are many examples of men who have known disgrace and then have ascended again. Churchill did. Lincoln did. So did MacArthur, Patton, Booker T. Washington, and Alfred the Great. Gandhi did also. As did King George VI of England. The list seems unending, and it can lead us to believe that greatness is not really possible without some early failure to overcome.

My favorite version of this kind of story will surprise you. It comes from the life of Mark the apostle. I love his tale because it is one of the most public in all of human history. It has to be—it's in the Bible! I love it also because, though it is right there on the pages of Scripture, it is revealed only in bits and pieces. Most people miss it completely. Mark's story also draws me because it is gritty, raw, and embarrassing. Nothing is kept from us, and I think this is a signal that we are supposed to take it all in and then live differently for having done so.

It is important for us to remember that Mark is among the greatest men in the history of Christianity. He is one of only four men who were privileged to write a gospel of Jesus Christ that ended up in the pages of the New Testament. He walked with giants like Peter and Paul. Early historians lauded him as a hero because of his gallant work in Egypt. He was also martyred, which gives him a holy and honored place in Christian memory. We should keep these later honors in mind as we ponder Mark's early years, a time when he was certainly anything but a hero.

We meet Mark in the pages of the Bible with these words: "A young man, wearing nothing but a linen garment, was following Jesus. When they seized him, he fled naked, leaving his garment behind" (Mark 14:51–52 NIV). I can't prove it definitely and scholars will debate it until the end of time, but I believe this young man is Mark. I believe these words are how Mark remembered this odd incident many decades after it occurred. He is thinking back upon the most terrifying, humiliating moment of his life. He wants us to see it just as it was.

We know a few things about Mark that help us understand this moment. He was from a wealthy family who owned a large home in Jerusalem. Jesus and his disciples often met there. In fact, the final Passover meal that Jesus ate with his disciples was likely eaten in an upper room of this home. As the early church gained its footing, believers met there regularly, and this is why, when Peter was released from King Herod's prison around AD 44, he went directly to Mark's house. He knew he would find fellow believers there (see Acts 12:12).

This might also explain why we meet Mark when he is wrapped only in a sheet and is fleeing soldiers. Since Jesus and his disciples likely ate the Last Supper at Mark's house, soldiers might well have been sent there to arrest Jesus after Judas betrayed him. The sound of men banging on the door of the house probably awakened Mark that night. Some scholars believe that he jumped up, wrapped himself quickly in his bedding, and ran to the place he knew Jesus would be: the grove surrounding a little olive press at the base of the Mount of Olives. Gethsemane.

When Mark arrived, soldiers had already captured Jesus. Mark watched for a moment and then realized he was in danger. Soldiers had already recognized him and were just trying to take him in hand. Naturally, Mark ran. One soldier nearly grabbed him but ended up with a handful of sheets. Mark scurried off into the night completely naked. Of course, he would never forget these moments. He saw Jesus

arrested. He abandoned the rabbi. He barely escaped capture by soldiers and had to make his way home naked. This was a joke to the
Romans, a scandal to the Jews, and a lasting humiliation to Mark. He
had been a coward that night, as had all of those who followed Jesus.

This is why Mark was the only author of a gospel to mention this
unusual episode in later years. It may also have been memorable to
him, though, because it was not the only time he ran away.

I said earlier that when Peter was released from prison, he went
to Mark's mother's house—to "the house of Mary, the mother of John,
also called Mark" as Luke describes it in Acts 12. The point is the
house belonged to Mark's mother. It doesn't seem there was a man
around—a husband or a father. He's absent. Scholars think Mark's
father was either dead by this time or he had become offended with
his wife's faith and left. Either way, young Mark was without a father.
This is important in light of what was about to take place.

It is also important to know that the Barnabas mentioned in the
New Testament is Mark's cousin. Originally Barnabas's name was
Joseph, but the disciples loved him so dearly they renamed him in the
loving, sometimes intimate way that men do. They stopped calling
him Joseph and instead gave him a name that meant "son of encouragement." That's the kind of man Barnabas was. Luke took pains to
say that Barnabas was "a good man, full of the Holy Spirit and faith"
(Acts 11:24 NIV).

This good man may have tried to be something of a surrogate
father to Mark. While Barnabas was doing important things in the
early days of the church—giving large sums of money, introducing the
newly converted Paul to the Christian leaders in Jerusalem, and serving the church as a trusted emissary—Mark was often at his cousin's
side. It was a privilege. It was also an opportunity to mature.

Finally, an even greater opportunity came Mark's way. The leaders
at Antioch commissioned Paul and Barnabas to break new ground for

the gospel in the pagan world. The two men decided to take Mark with them. What an opportunity this was! Mark was granted the honored position of assisting the most important emissaries of Christ in the world at the time. It was the privilege of a lifetime.

But watch: Paul and Barnabas set out immediately to fulfill their commission. We read of their departure in Acts 13:4. They made their way to the island of Cyprus and proclaimed the gospel there for a short while, perhaps as much as a few weeks. It went well at first, but then we read this in Acts 13:13: "Paul and his companions sailed to Perga in Pamphylia, where John [Mark] left them to return to Jerusalem" (NIV).

What? Why? What happened? Mark didn't make it even *eight verses*!

Unfortunately, we don't know why. Maybe Mark didn't like carrying the luggage or making the Starbucks run. Maybe he missed his mommy. Or perhaps Paul was too demanding. Mark may have yearned for his air conditioning or his big-screen TV or time to chat with friends on Facebook. Who knows? Whatever happened, Mark abandoned Paul and Barnabas. Everyone knew it too.

Keep watching now: Paul and Barnabas finished their journey and returned to Antioch. Before long there was a big stir about the Gentiles who were becoming Christians. The big question was whether they had to become Jews first. Did they have to be circumcised and live under the conditions of the law before they could follow Jesus? All the church leaders met in Jerusalem to iron these things out. Paul and Barnabas testified about their ministry to the Gentiles at this meeting in order to help the apostles decide the matter. All ended well.

This is when Barnabas made his big mistake. He suggested to Paul that they should return to the churches they planted on their previous journey. Paul eagerly agreed. Then Barnabas suggested that they take Mark with them again.

Paul was a great man but he could also be impatient and harsh. He was no "son of encouragement." When Barnabas suggested they take Mark, Paul erupted. Luke, the author of the book of Acts, tells us that Paul and Barnabas had a "sharp dispute." This is code language. What it means is that the two men had a fight. They argued, it got loud, it went on for some time, and things were said.

Remember that Mark is Barnabas's cousin. Remember that Paul doesn't care. The little twerp had betrayed them right at the start of their last journey and Paul had no intention of trusting him again. Mark was an immature mama's boy and a sissy. There was no place for a weakling in the important work Paul and Barnabas were called to do. That's what Paul argued, anyway.

What happened? Paul and Barnabas parted company angrily. Barnabas took Mark and went back to his home in Crete. Paul chose a man named Silas to work with, and the two struck off in a different direction. Luke tells us that Paul was "commended by the brothers" (Acts 15:40 ESV). This is also code language. It means the church leaders backed Paul.

Here is the tragedy. Paul and Barnabas never worked together again. The Holy Spirit had specifically told the church at Antioch to commission the two men as a team. They made one journey together and then parted company forever. And it was all because of Mark. The devastation is hard to watch. Barnabas is never mentioned again in the New Testament except as a memory. The early church is distracted and divided over the matter. The Holy Spirit's express purposes are never fulfilled, at least never fulfilled by Paul and Barnabas as a team. It was a full-scale crisis for the early Christians and, again, it was all because Mark was too spoiled and immature to do his duty. The churches all over the Roman Empire knew about his failure too. Once again, people said, Mark had run away.

There could hardly be a larger failure than this. This seemingly small matter of a self-centered, undisciplined man threatened to divide the early church, hinder the Holy Spirit, and limit the evangelistic reach of God's people. People thanked God that Paul had known what to do when Barnabas couldn't see past his family biases.

This is where it all might have ended: with Mark's name a byword for *spoiled brat* and *man of no spirit*.

It did not end in this tragic state, though, and to know why, we have to let our minds run to Crete. We don't know exactly what happened there, but we can fit a few pieces together. We can be fairly sure that Mark came to regret his foolishness. Barnabas, ever the encourager, would have mentored his young cousin. He trained Mark and helped him become more the man he was destined to be. Something significant began to happen in Mark's life. He became useful, trustworthy. His character changed, his understanding deepened. He became more like Jesus and less like the pleasure-seeking pagan world.

We get some sense of how much Mark had changed when nearly fifteen years after the initial crisis the church at Colossae came across these words in one of Paul's letters. "My fellow prisoner Aristarchus sends you his greetings, as does Mark, the cousin of Barnabas" (Colossians 4:10 NIV).

What? Mark is back? What's happened? We don't know exactly. What we do know is that Paul was writing from a prison in the city of Rome and Mark was with him. Mark had returned from Crete and, obviously, had reconciled with Paul. Just after this first mention of Mark, Paul wrote, "You have received instructions about him; if he comes to you, welcome him" (v. 10). Clearly, Paul wanted the believers who were offended with Mark to open their hearts to him again. This must have been encouraging to hear throughout the churches. The season of bitterness had passed.

It gets even better. Sometime after his return and after the churches embraced him again, Mark must have served with Peter, because in 1 Peter 5:13, Peter refers to Mark as his "son." Scholars believe that

Mark's gospel gives evidence of Peter's influence, which means the two men may have served the Lord together for years on end, with Mark absorbing Peter's memories of what it was like to walk at Jesus' side.

All of this is heartening to witness, but then comes the tender conclusion. Years later, Paul is once again in a Roman prison, though not in "his own rented house" as he was during his first imprisonment (see Acts 28:30 NIV). Instead, he is in a dank, filthy hole in the ground where the Romans held the worst of prisoners. From this hellhole, Paul wrote his final letter, his second to Timothy. We can hear the final tone in his words, and we sense that he is preparing the churches for his death. He was wise to do this. He was likely executed not too many months after he wrote it.

So in the last chapter of the last letter Paul would ever write, we read these words: "Get Mark and bring him with you, because he is helpful to me in my ministry" (2 Timothy 4:11 NIV).

How much these words mean! How they reveal the change in both men and the triumph of forgiveness and grace. And how much the words must have meant to Mark's still-bruised soul.

The story has progressed a great distance from the days when Paul and Barnabas fought angrily over whether to forgive Mark and take him on their second journey. Now, after all these years, Paul finds Mark helpful. Paul has mellowed, but then, Mark is no longer the complaining, unstable man/child who left the apostles he was assigned to serve—and after only *eight verses*!

Even this is not the end, though. You see, Mark had failed and failed horribly, but then he did what true men do: he gave himself to the changes his failures called for. He submitted to mentoring by Barnabas, then he risked presenting himself to Paul. They then reconciled. Finally, he served faithfully at Peter's side. Unlike that first humiliating journey, Mark became a teachable man, a man who would do whatever he had to in order to live down his shame and repair the damage done.

We learn from the pages of early church historians that Mark eventually became the bishop of Alexandria. We are told he led his people well. We know, too, that a fierce wave of persecution washed over the Alexandrian church and Mark was ultimately killed. There is a tradition that tells us people honored this great man by saying, "This time, he did not run away."

I cannot think of a more moving story of failure and restoration than this one from the life of Mark. That it is from the pages of the Bible and that it challenges some of our assumptions about the ideal of the first-century church makes me love it even more.

Mark's story is for both men and women, of course, but it touches me most as a window into some of what it means to be a man. Life in this fallen world is risky and dangerous. Losses will come. Failures will happen. Our journey will not be a constant, joyful, upward ascent.

Because of what a man is meant to be for his family, his society, and his God, he cannot allow failure and loss to destroy him. He should live knowing that such seasons are possible, and he should have a firm grasp on the truth that will help him rebuild.

First, he has to know he is destined. He can rise again from any depth of destruction because he knows his life is defined by something more powerful than his own sin or stupidity. It is powered by the purpose determined for him by his God.

Second, he has to acknowledge his folly. Call it repentance. Call it "hanging a lantern on your weaknesses." Call it brokenness or humility. Whatever we call it, realizing we are not as we should be and that hiding this fact only deepens the devastation is one of the great principles of turning around a damaged life.

Third, submit to more capable men. We do not have all the resources we need even in the best of times. We certainly don't have what we need in seasons of failure and embarrassment. We have to have mentors, coaches, trainers, and fathers. We need men who don't fear us and are tough enough to press painful truths into our lives. We can't rebuild without them.

Finally, we will have to face those we've damaged. We cannot run. Many of the men I have worked with during their potentially life-defining failures have had to fight the temptation to run from the ruin every single day. It is essential in reclaiming your lost territory that you stay in that territory—despite the mountains of rubble you've created—and yield to the processes of both God and man that are designed to help you reclaim and rebuild.

Mark is one of my heroes. He was a manly man. Sure, he was one of the great saints of the church, but before that he was a knucklehead who did great damage when the Christian faith was just starting to spread out into the world. He responded with humility and courage, though, and ended up changing the world.

Now *that* is what a man does.

WHAT THEN WILL YOU DO?
HOW WILL YOU SHOW YOURSELF A MAN?

1. Think carefully over your life and list the failures that have been significant to you. Can you see patterns to these failures? Are there character flaws common among them? What do they tell you about yourself and about your weaknesses?

2. Is there anyone you should reconcile with because of your failures? Is there anything you should confess? Is there anything you have taken that you should restore?

3. If you do not think you have completely overcome after your failures, find some wise older men and submit the matter to them. Ask for their help not only in rebuilding your outer life and reputation life, but also in helping you build the character of a genuine man.

4. With the help of your mentors, define what rebuilding or overcoming after your failure would look like. How can you live out a positive history on the very ground where you once failed? Turn this to prayer and remain open to opportunities for victory on the very site of your defeat.

5. Finally, consider how you will respond differently should another season of failure or devastation befall you. In other words, how does a manly man, a genuine man, face loss and devastation?

"FAR BETTER IT IS TO DARE MIGHTY THINGS,
TO WIN GLORIOUS TRIUMPHS, EVEN THOUGH
CHECKERED BY FAILURE, THAN TO TAKE
RANK WITH THOSE POOR SPIRITS WHO
NEITHER ENJOY NOR SUFFER TOO MUCH,
BECAUSE THEY LIVE IN THE GRAY TWILIGHT
THAT KNOWS NOT VICTORY NOR DEFEAT."

—*Theodore Roosevelt, in his speech "The Strenuous Life, A
Speech before the Hamilton Club," Chicago, April 10, 1899*

OPPORTUNITY

This I beheld, or dreamed it in a dream:—
There spread a cloud of dust along a plain;
And underneath the cloud, or in it, raged
A furious battle, and men yelled, and swords
Shocked upon swords and shields. A prince's banner
Wavered, then staggered backward, hemmed by foes.
A craven hung along the battle's edge,
And thought, "Had I a sword of keener steel—
That blue blade that the king's son bears,—but this
Blunt thing—!" he snapped and flung it from his hand,
And lowering crept away and left the field.
Then came the king's son, wounded, sore bestead,
And weaponless, and saw the broken sword,
Hilt-buried in the dry and trodden sand,
And ran and snatched it, and with battle shout
Lifted afresh he hewed his enemy down,
And saved a great cause that heroic day.

—EDWARD ROWLAND SILL

SELF-EDUCATION

If we asked men today to list the duties or disciplines that comprise true manhood, most would not include learning or the acquisition of knowledge. This signals a tragic failure to understand the traits that make a great man. The truth is most great men in history have become great because they aggressively pursued knowledge. They overcame gaps in their early education. They studied to understand the world at a level well beyond their years. They took responsibility for their education and did not wait for the knowledge they needed to come to them.

There isn't the space here to list all the great men who set themselves apart through self-education. Just a few examples will suffice. Winston Churchill read so ravenously when he was a young officer in India that a biographer later wrote that "he became his own university."[17] Lincoln was also enflamed by a hunger to learn. He read every book he could buy or borrow on the Illinois frontier, enlisted tutors, followed lecturers from town to town and worked late into many a night to master a philosophy, understand a mathematical formula, or memorize a poem. Benjamin Franklin taught himself five languages and formed a junto of young Philadelphia journeymen who met regularly to teach each other in hopes of rising in society. Thomas Jefferson taught himself seven languages, including Arabic. These and hundreds of other prominent men first distinguished themselves through ambitious programs of self-education.

This devotion to learning is more vital today than ever. We live at a time when the amount of knowledge in the world doubles every five years or so. There is a technological revolution approximately every eighteen to twenty-four months. This is so established that experts call it Moore's Law, and more than a few think the revolution occurs in something more like twelve to eighteen months. To put the amount of knowledge in our world into perspective, the average man living in the high Middle Ages only needed to possess as much knowledge as is contained in one Sunday edition of the *New York Times*. Think of how many times that amount we need to know today.

There is also the matter of how knowledge becomes obsolete. I remember clearly how my college roommate filled our dorm room with computer paper while he tried to master Fortran and Cobalt, computer languages his professors assured him he would need to know. I remember him slaving late into the night with other business majors, all terrified they would not succeed if they did not know how to use these systems with skill.

We graduated together in 1981. That was the year of the first personal computer. Within months of getting his degree, my roommate's hard-earned knowledge became obsolete. Through the years since, he had to learn new ways of computing over and over again to become the successful Los Angeles businessman he is today. He did not go back to school to learn these new methods. He taught himself, repeatedly, using skills not all of his peers possessed.

Devotion to self-education is unquestionably one of the marks of an exceptional man. Passive men wait for knowledge to come to them. Weak men assume what they need to know will seek them out. Men of great character and drive search out the knowledge they need. They take responsibility for knowing what they must know to live effectively in their generation and to prosper. I know this sounds old school. I know this sounds like a lesson meant for the barefoot boy born in a dirt-floor cabin in the 1800s. I assure you it is a lesson for men today. In fact, it may prove to be one of the most important lessons for men today.

No one exemplifies this in recent history like Harry Truman, the only president of the twentieth century who did not have a college degree. He would serve as a county judge, a US senator, Franklin Roosevelt's vice president, and, ultimately, president of the United States for many years, and, whatever criticism might have been hurled at him, no one thought him too ignorant to fill these roles. Yet most of what he knew he had learned on his own in a lifelong project of self-education.

In his youth, Truman almost perfectly fulfilled the stereotype of the bespectacled, undersized, sickly child. When he was eight he was diagnosed with a severe eye disease. At nine, he contracted diphtheria, which left him paralyzed for months. He passed the time by reading through thick, clouded glasses that friends said made him look like an irritated owl.

He devoured Charles Francis Horne's *Great Men and Famous Women*, Plutarch's *Lives*, and Caesar's *Commentaries*. This was reading well beyond his years, but it set him on a journey into the world of books. "I always had my nose stuck in a book, history books mostly. There were about three thousand books in the library downtown, and I guess I read them all, including the encyclopedias. I'm embarrassed to say that I remember what I read too."[18]

This was more than a bookish phase in the life of a lonely boy. The knowledge books granted him became a mandate to think and reason for himself. It made Truman an independent thinker, a boy—and

then, ultimately, a man—who sought out ideas and perspectives often removed from the school curriculum and the intellectual consensus of his day. In his typically crusty manner, Truman explained this departure from the mainstream: "The thing I found out from reading was there is damn little information in most schoolbooks worth a damn. If you wanted to find out why France was against England during the Revolution and the why and wherefore of Jefferson's being able to buy Louisiana, you had to go look it up for yourself. It didn't matter how good your teachers were. They never taught you things like that."[19]

His reading caused him to suspect bias in writers, particularly among historians—"Historians editorializing is in the same class as the modern irresponsible columnist. So study men, not historians."[20] And this moved him to read the writings of the men who made history. He eagerly consumed books like the *Autobiography of Benjamin Franklin*, Thomas Jefferson's *Notes on Virginia*, Ulysses S. Grant's *Memoirs*, the *Meditations* of Marcus Aurelius, the works of Cicero, and the writings of Cato, William Sherman, Montesquieu, and George Washington. He made memoirs and autobiographies his intellectual diet and in later years often knew more about the great men of history than scholars who had only read writings about these men and not the writings of the men themselves.

This devotion to reading and to searching out knowledge on his own set Truman apart from other men of his time. At a time when secularizing trends meant religion was seldom emphasized in schools, even as a force of history, Truman knew the role religion had played in the world and found himself instructing far more institutionally educated men. In a meeting with numerous eminent ambassadors, he once sketched out the differences between the major religions of the world on a napkin, impressing—and educating—men with degrees from Harvard and Yale. He thought nothing of explaining the meaning of constitutional principles over dinner or describing during a game of cards how geography contributed to the crises of his administration.

For Truman, knowledge was not something removed from life. It was interwoven with life, an interpreter of life, perhaps even the earthly power behind life. He did not rely on society to provide this knowledge. He roared after it, dug it out on his own, and did not rest until he understood what he needed to understand in order to live and to lead.

Historians have often treated Truman's unique self-education as a minor feature of a minor president. Yet during his presidency, Truman was forced to contend with the end of World War II; the Korean War; the dawn of the atomic age; the crisis of General Douglas MacArthur and civilian rule of the military; the founding of the United Nations; the birth of the nation of Israel; the spread of communism; a series of steel, coal, and rail strikes that nearly paralyzed the nation; the rise of McCarthyism; an assassination attempt; and racial equality in the armed services—among hundreds of other critical issues. He approached each of these crises believing that "there is nothing new in the world except the history you don't know."[21] This belief left him with valuable perspective on each of these crises and helped him craft the principled approach to leadership that marked his years in office.

It was all fruit of his own passionate pursuit of knowledge, a pursuit not of the classroom but of the curious man consumed with the written word. Truman had read, pondered, applied, and learned. He had distilled wisdom from his years of reading and applied this wisdom as directly as any president in American history.

A publisher once asked the thirty-third president if he read himself to sleep. "No, young man," said Truman, "I like to read myself awake."[22]

This is a good moment to remember one of Mansfield's Manly Maxims: "Manly men tend their fields." It means that we take care of the lives and property entrusted to us. It means that we take responsibility for everything in the "field assigned to us."

We cannot do this without knowledge. We cannot do it if we are ignorant of our times, blind to the trends shaping our lives, and oblivious to the basic knowledge that allows us to do what we are called to do as men. We must know enough about law, health, science, economics, politics, and technology to fulfill our roles. We should also know enough about our faith to stand our ground in a secular age, resist heresies, and teach our families. We also shouldn't be without the benefits of literature and poetry, of good novels and stirring stories, all of which make us more relevant and more effective.

We need all of this, and no one is going to force it upon us. Nor will we acquire what we need from a degree program or a study group alone, as valuable as these can be. The truth is that men who aspire to be genuine men and serve well have no choice: they must devote themselves to an aggressive program of self-education. They have to read books, stay current with websites and periodicals, consult experts, and put themselves in a position to know.

It isn't as hard as it sounds, particularly in our Internet age. Much of what a man needs to know can land in his iPad while he is sleeping, but he has to know enough to value this power in the first place.

To ignore this duty can mean disaster. How many men have lost jobs because they did not see massive trends on the horizon? How many men have failed to stay intellectually sharp and so gave up ground in their professions to others with more active minds? How many have lost money through uninformed investments or have not taken opportunities in expanding fields or have missed promotions because they had not bothered to learn about new technologies or what changes social media, for example, would bring to their jobs?

I do not want to be negative. Learning is a joy. Reading is one of the great pleasures of life. A man ought to invest in knowledge because it is part of living in this world fully engaged and glorifying God. Yet our times also make it essential. The amount of knowledge in the world is increasing. Technology is transforming our lives. New trends can rise like floodwaters and sweep devastation into our homes. Men committed to tending their fields learn, study, research, dig out facts, and test theories. They know how to safeguard their families. They serve well because they serve as informed men.

WHAT THEN WILL YOU DO?
HOW WILL YOU SHOW YOURSELF A MAN?

1. Look back upon your own educational life. What has been positive? Where have you learned the most and enjoyed it? Then, what has been negative in your educational career? Have you been turned off to reading? Did you fail in some way or sustain a wound that left you believing you could not learn the knowledge you need in this life? Confront these issues in prayer, with friends and leaders, and with your spouse. Determine not to let any painful experience of the past keep you from "tending your field."

2. Take inventory of your life and determine areas of knowledge in which you are weak. Identify teachers, websites, books, video series—anything that will help you learn. Don't be too proud to use books like *American Government for Dummies* or *The Complete Idiot's Guide to Accounting.* Series like these are wonderfully helpful and, frankly, I've met with leading lawyers who had *Constitutional Law for Dummies* hidden in their briefcases. Get the knowledge you need. Don't be ashamed.

3. Work to change the intellectual culture in your home. Turn off the television and make sure there are books in abundance. Studies show that the mere presence of books in a home raises the intellectual activity of those who live there. Help protect your wife's time so she can read at leisure. Schedule reading nights for your family, even reading contests. And don't be beyond bribing your children to read.

Wouldn't ten dollars a book be a fantastic investment in a child's future? Always be aware of your example. Nothing will inspire your children to read and learn like seeing you doing it first.

4. Be systematic. Have a long-term plan. Collect recommended reading lists in various fields and make sure to include some of the classics in your lifetime reading plan. Subscribe to podcasts in your field and any field in which you need an upgrade. Set goals of a certain number of books a month or a year, and urge friends to hold you accountable.

5. Remember not to panic. This is the work of a lifetime. Just beginning is already a form of success.

"TOMORROW'S ILLITERATE WILL NOT BE THE MAN WHO CAN'T READ; HE WILL BE THE MAN WHO HAS NOT LEARNED HOW TO LEARN."

—*Alvin Toffler, from* Future Shock *(1970)*

WILDNESS

On a Sunday in the late 1870s, a teenager sporting a black eye sheepishly joined his Sunday school class at Christ Church in Boston. As he entered the room, the other students in the class whispered to each other and wondered what their teacher would do when he saw the spreading bruise. When he arrived moments later, the teacher saw what had happened and knew better than to add to the young man's humiliation. Instead, he casually asked about the black eye. The boy explained that a bully much bigger than he was had been pinching his sister. Despite repeated requests, the bully refused to stop. Finally, the smaller boy knew he had to come to his sister's defense and he soon found himself in a fight. Thus the black eye.

The students watched wide-eyed. In upper-class Boston, fighting wasn't condoned. The sons of the elite did not brawl, particularly sons of families that attended Christ Church, which sat a short distance from prestigious Harvard University. Surely the teacher would chastise the young man and perhaps ban him from the class.

The students were stunned to hear the teacher tell the young man he had done the right thing. Sometimes violence served righteous ends and defending a sister's honor certainly qualified. After further discussion, the teacher gave the boy a dollar and commended his valor to the class.

When members of the church's board heard of this, they were incensed. A teacher at Christ Church encouraging one of its boys to fight in the streets like a vagrant? No. The board had to put a stop to this. A vote was called and the teacher was told that he had gone too far. He was fired. The board asked him not to return.

The teacher left and returned to his studies at Harvard. He had no regrets. He had given good counsel. His name was Theodore Roosevelt.

This story is particularly revealing given that Theodore Roosevelt later became an American symbol of "the strenuous life," one of his favorite phrases. He believed in hard work, in pushing the body, in living on the aggressive, muscular, energetic side of life. He worried that his generation of men were going soft and that the body would rob the mind and then the manhood of the nation. He was right to be concerned.

Yet how had the son of a wealthy New York family come to learn such lessons, to know the value of a life that came more naturally from the frontier than the "sissified" East?

It is true Theodore Roosevelt was born in 1858 to the fineries of New York's upper class. His childhood was filled with family tours of Europe, with scurrying servants tending a huge Main Street house—in 1865, young Teddy leaned out a front window to see the funeral procession of Abraham Lincoln pass by—and with the services of expensive tutors. All was not well, though. He was tormented by an asthma of a severe, life-deforming kind.

Eminent historian David McCullough described this torment in his biography of Roosevelt entitled *Mornings on Horseback*.

The attacks, when they come are a shattering, numbing experience—always, no matter how many times it happened before. Nights

are made a shambles, sleep is lost, nerves are frayed. Parents become intensely wary of anything that might bring on an attack. They grow increasingly protective, often engulfing in their good intentions. And if, as the years go by, the child shows no improvement, they begin feeling desperate and depleted; they see themselves caught in the grip of something altogether beyond comprehension and their ability to cope. Some mothers "just about go crazy" with worry.[23]

This was the childhood of Theodore Roosevelt. He was an intelligent child with a fierce curiosity and zeal for investigating life, but his body failed him. Exertions brought on breathlessness, which left him weak and bedridden. Even when he paced himself, he quickly ran out of energy. He seemed doomed to a nearly housebound life. Neighbors whispered that it was good the Roosevelts were rich. This son might never be able to work.

Finally, his father intervened. He had paid for every kind of innovative treatment—sulfur baths and massages and odd therapies involving electricity. Nothing worked. Finally, he relied on the spirit of his boy. In September of 1870, he sat "Thee" down but used his son's full name rather than the family's pet name. "Theodore, you have the mind, but you have not the body, and without the help of the body, the mind cannot go as far as it should. You must make your body. It is hard drudgery to make one's body, but I know you will do it."[24]

It was a turning point. What boy wishes to disappoint his father? What boy does not take to heart his father's solution to a life-altering challenge?

A family member who watched this conversation later said that young Theodore, "the sorry little specimen," looked up at his father, "threw back his head and declared he would do it."[25]

It was just the kind of challenge to better himself against a defining impediment that has made many exceptional men. Theodore devoted himself completely. He lifted weights, hammered away at punching bags, swung dumbbells, and spent hours grunting himself into position on the horizontal bars.

Yet years went by and there was little improvement. His parents tried to hide their disappointment when he proudly showed them a new, adolescent muscle or a move he had mastered on the bars. It was still pitiful, as was his vastly undersized, near emaciated body.

He didn't stop, though. He lifted and punched and strained for years. Finally, in his freshman year at Harvard, he began catching up. McCullough has written, "The picture that emerges, sketchy as it may be, is of an almost miraculous transformation." It is incorrect to believe that Roosevelt defeated asthma with exercise. He would suffer asthmatic episodes for the rest of his life. Yet it is not going too far to say that his exercise regimen contributed to the grand reversal of ill health he enjoyed in his freshman year. It is also not going too far to say that those dreary years of exercise, hour after hour each day, made him into a man who knew the power of work, of will over body, and of the need for a man to live a strenuous life. Those years taught Theodore more than he could actually live out, but the day would come when all he had learned would rescue him.

Roosevelt's public story is well known. He would graduate from Harvard and soon after enter the New York state legislature. A naval history he had started in college, *The Naval War of 1812*, was published in 1882 and earned him wide acclaim. He was appointed the US civil service commissioner in 1889, resigned to become president of the New York police board, and in 1897 was appointed assistant secretary of the navy by President McKinley. He led a volunteer unit in the Spanish-American War, returned a war hero, and was elected governor of New York. He served in that role until 1900, when he became McKinley's vice-presidential nominee. The ticket was victorious. On September 6, 1901, McKinley was shot. When the president succumbed to his wounds on September 14, Theodore Roosevelt became president of the United States. He was forty-two years old.

His writings, vision, and grand personality would endear him to his generation. His energy and triumphant spirit would also leave an imprint upon his age. Yet none of it would have been possible had he not known how to recover from the worst day of tragedy in his life.

It was February 14, 1884—Valentine's Day. Theodore was in Albany tending the business of the legislature. His wife, Alice, was pregnant and distracted by plans for their new home on Long Island's Oyster Bay. Theodore's mother lived with the young couple as well. She was a comfort, for Alice's pregnancy had not been smooth and she had been forced to remain in bed for weeks on end. When the child finally came on February 12, all danger seemed to have passed. Everyone was consumed with the beautiful new baby girl who graced their lives.

Theodore was called back to Albany soon after and this is when the trouble began. On the morning of the thirteenth, he received a telegram that the baby was fine and healthy but that the mother was "only fairly well." Within a few hours, he received word he should return home immediately. When he finally reached home, his distraught brother met him. "There is a curse on this house," Eliot Roosevelt declared. "Mother is dying and Alice is dying too."[26] It was true. Alice was dying of Bright's disease, a severe renal ailment, and Theodore's mother, Martha Roosevelt, had fallen ill with what proved to be the final stages of typhoid.

The scene that unfolded was one of the most horrid ever to befall a future president. Both the people he loved most in the world, his mother and his wife, were dying on the same day and in the same house. Roosevelt rushed up and down stairs between the two women for many hours—praying, tending, and simply holding limp bodies in his arms when there was nothing more to do. His mother died shortly after midnight. His wife died the next afternoon. Two days later, Theodore Roosevelt sat in a pew at New York's Fifth Avenue Presbyterian Church and endured a double funeral. The next day, at the same church, he participated in the baptism of Alice Lee Roosevelt, his new daughter. He would write of these days, "The light has gone out of my life."[27]

He was destroyed. Death filled his home. He might have thrown himself into politics as an escape, but his Republican Party had already ceased being his home, its machinations and corruption demoralizing him. His baby daughter held his affection, but she was in need of a woman's care.

What Roosevelt did at that moment in his life scandalized many in New York society but it completed the process of making him a heroic man. He handed his beloved daughter to his sister, sold nearly everything he had, and moved to the Dakota Territories, where for several years he had been investing in a cattle ranch that overlooked a bend in the Missouri River. He would remain there for three years.

Why did he go? Why such a dramatic move?

The answer seems to be that Roosevelt needed to restore and rebuild and he knew only one way to do it: return to the strenuous and the difficult. Perhaps those hours of lifting weights and balancing on horizontal bars had surfaced forces of soul he needed to summon once again. Perhaps a return to an arduous physical life was the only way he knew to quell the turmoil in his heart. Obviously, he needed space, wilderness, difficult tasks, and looming danger. He knew this was the key to healing. He had experienced this truth in his life before.

After arriving in the Dakotas, Roosevelt did not spend three years in a comfortable chair by the fire with a brandy in one hand and a book in the other. Instead, he became the western hero of his dreams. He herded cattle and broke bucking horses. He stood down grizzlies and fought off desperadoes. On one occasion, he tracked thieves for three days across three hundred miles in subzero temperatures. Once he took the criminals captive, he then traveled another six days and one hundred fifty miles to surrender them to authorities.

And the wildness healed him. He tamed the wilderness around him by way of taming the wilderness of his own soul. He grieved and got through it. He lived in the moment, in the physical, and in intimate connection with nature. It forced him from living entirely in his thoughts to living a rooted, earthy life in which thoughts come only after work is done.

He wrote during these years, and reviewers lauded his work as "masculine, fervid and innovative."[28] Over time, he helped create the literature of the Wild West. He was living what he wrote before he wrote it, though, and this made him authentic, not just as a public man but, more importantly, to himself. It gave him a brand of confidence and insight that marked him the rest of his life.

Roosevelt would return to the East. He would accomplish many things. Never would he forget the Dakota years. Listen to how he later described his memories of this time.

In after years there shall ever come to mind the memory of endless prairies shimmering in the bright sun; of vast, snow-clad wastes, lying and desolate under gray skies; of the melancholy marshes; of the rush of mighty rivers; of the breath of the evergreen forest in summer; of the crooning of ice-armored pines at the touch of the winds of winter; of cataracts roaring between hoary mountain passes; of all the innumerable sights and sounds of the wilderness and of the silences that brood in its still depths.[29]

Look carefully at these words. It is obvious that the land became more than something physical to him. It became an incarnation of his grieving soul. Wastes. Desolate. Melancholy. Brood. This is how

Roosevelt experienced the land. It had somehow taken on the form of his inner world. To work the land was to clear the entangled scrub brush of his soul. To break a horse or turn trees into sturdy barns and bunkhouses was to make the raw and wounding into a place a man could peacefully live. This is what happened to Theodore Roosevelt in those essential Dakota years.

The man who would become the twenty-sixth president of the United States endured extreme tragedy and needed an extreme experience to deliver him of his grief. Yet all men need what Roosevelt found—a strenuous physical life, the possibility of harm, challenges to face, enemies to oppose, land to conquer. Our lives push us away from this. We work in cubicles or comfortable vehicles. Technology serves us and keeps us from exertion. We live in an opulent blandness—overfed, overtended, overentertained, and overly preoccupied with ourselves.

But men need aggressive physical lives. They need contest and conquest, strain and struggle. Otherwise, we lose ourselves to soft-ness and effeminacy. It is not much of a surprise that a New Testament word that is translated *effeminate* from the original Greek actually means "soft through luxury." It is a warning.

Most of us will not spend three years breaking horses and hunting down thieves in the snow. Nor should we. Still, we can let Theodore Roosevelt's example remind us that we are not disembodied spirits. We are souls sealed into bodies. We need to work the machinery, be alive in both body and soul.

It will awaken the masculinity in us. It will help us to untangle our inner knots. It will remind us that we are men. Perhaps the women and children in our lives are waiting for this, waiting for us to recover ourselves. This alone would be worth the battle.

WHAT THEN WILL YOU DO?
HOW WILL YOU SHOW YOURSELF A MAN?

1. Discuss Theodore Roosevelt's story with friends. What portions seem similar to experiences you've had? How did the "strenuous life" answer Roosevelt's inner needs in the areas you identify with?

2. Evaluate your current physical life. Do you have arenas of controlled combat? Do you have "combat" and "struggle" in your life, even if it is twice a week at the gym? Do you have space, territory, wilds that you enter at least occasionally?

3. John Eldredge has said in his masterful *Wild at Heart* that Adam was made in the wilderness, and Eve was made in a garden. This, he suggests, contributes to some of the differences between men and women and also some of their different needs. Look up the stories of Adam and Eve. Do you think Eldredge is right? If so, what does it mean for you?

4. How are the young men in your life exhibiting their need for wildness, for frontier or adventure? Let me ask this question through a brief story. When my son was about ten years old, he got caught lying in the middle of a street late one night. He later explained that he was trying to see how close he would let the cars get to him before jumping up and running to the curb. Fortunately, the policeman who "arrested" Jonathan was a friend of mine and brought him to me to inform me that Jonathan was going to prison. Of course, my muscular SWAT commander friend was winking behind Jonathan's back. Jonathan was terrified. My fierce-looking buddy was tossing

hand cuffs in the air with one hand while fingering his holstered gun with his other hand. I took my son into "custody," assuring Officer Apollo Creed that I would deal with the boy. I have to say, though, that I knew what my son was doing. He was testing himself. He wanted to know if he was any kind of man. I had to laugh, but only after I descended on him like the wrath of God.

Is anything of this kind happening in your home? Is some controlled wildness called for?

5. Finally, Eleanor Roosevelt advised us to "Do something everyday that scares you." Don't just respond to this chapter by getting a membership to the gym or buying a big, ugly piece of home exercise equipment. And *do not* think you are a wild man because you have a hunting lease that lets you sit in an air-conditioned blind fitted out with recliner, fridge, and satellite TV. *No!* Do a tandem jump out of an airplane. Hang glide. Train to hike to the summit of a mountain. Scuba dive. Go work a friend's ranch. Don't be stupid, but do press the boundaries. And get your buddies to hold you accountable so you don't wimp out. We all have that potential.

> ## "HE WAS MASTERED BY THE SHEER SURGING OF LIFE, THE TIDAL WAVE OF BEING, THE PERFECT JOY OF EACH SEPARATE MUSCLE, JOINT, AND SINEW IN THAT IT WAS EVERYTHING THAT WAS NOT DEATH, THAT IT WAS AGLOW AND RAMPANT, EXPRESSING ITSELF IN MOVEMENT, FLYING EXULTANTLY UNDER THE STARS."
>
> —*Jack London, from* The Call of the Wild *(1903)*

THE PRAYER OF SIR FRANCIS DRAKE

Disturb us, Lord, when
We are too well pleased with ourselves,
When our dreams have come true
Because we have dreamed too little,
When we arrived safely
Because we sailed too close to the shore.

Disturb us, Lord, when
With the abundance of things we possess
We have lost our thirst
For the waters of life;
Having fallen in love with life,
We have ceased to dream of eternity
And in our efforts to build a new earth,
We have allowed our vision
Of the new Heaven to dim.

Disturb us, Lord, to dare more boldly,
To venture on wider seas
Where storms will show your mastery;
Where losing sight of land,
We shall find the stars.

We ask You to push back
The horizons of our hopes;
And to push into the future
In strength, courage, hope, and love.

—SIR FRANCIS DRAKE

INTEGRITY

OUR GENERATION HEARS THE WORD *INTEGRITY*, AND IT SEEMS to mean "honest and good." A man of integrity is a man who won't steal or lie. We pick this up just from hearing the way the word is commonly used. It takes our understanding a bit further, though, to know the word *integrity* is related to the word *integrate*. Both come from the Latin word *integras*, which means "soundness, wholeness or entire."

The army of ancient Rome used this word almost daily in its inspection ritual. A commander would walk the line of legionnaires, inspecting each man to confirm that he was fit for duty. As the commander came before one of his men, the soldier would sweep his fist hard into the middle of his chest, just over his heart, and shout "Integras!" The commander first listened for that rich, full quality of a healthy soldier's voice and then he listened for the clang that well-kept armor would emit when struck. The two sounds—the man's voice and the condition of his armor—confirmed the integrity of the soldier.

The word indicates soundness through and through. We sometimes hear people say things like, "Cut that boy anywhere and he bleeds Texas." This is close to the meaning of integrity. A man isn't healthy if he is sound in one part of his body or life and unsound in another part. He's only healthy, true, and noble if he is all these things in all that he is.

This broader definition of integrity has always come to my mind when I think of the ancient story of Job. Now most people don't like the story of Job. It seems too depressing to them. Perhaps it scares them a bit to think of a God who can take away all a man has any moment he chooses. Besides, the book of Job is long, preachy, and filled with angry guys arguing by the hour. It's not usually on anyone's list of "Favorite Books of the Bible."

I'm fascinated by this man Job, though. I'm moved by how he stood his ground and took his dissent just as far as righteousness allowed but no further. Let me tell a quick version of his story and then I'll tell you how I think Job illustrates seven principles all manly men need to know.

We know only a few things about Job, but they are all we need. He lived in the land of Uz, which was east of the Jordan River and included regions like Edom and Aram. It is likely he lived in the second millennium BC (2000 to 1000 BC), and we are told he lived to be more than one hundred years old, like many of the other patriarchs of Israel. He was wealthy, he was devoted to God, and he served as priest for his family, praying and making sacrifices for them.

And God was proud of him. When the angels of heaven were passing by the throne on one occasion, God pointed Job out specifically, describing him as an "upright" man who "shuns evil."

Satan was among the angels who heard this and thought that God was being a bit disingenuous. *Well, of course Job serves you. You've protected him and made him fabulously wealthy. Take it all away and he'll curse you to your face.*

Scholars will debate until the end of time whether this actually happened, why it happened, and whether it happened this way if it did happen. We'll stick with the story on the page, which tells us that God hears Satan's taunts and decides to put his servant Job to the test. He tells Satan he can strike all Job's property but not Job himself.

And so it begins. Just about the worst day any man in the history of the world has ever had begins to unfold. An enemy tribe steals Job's donkeys and oxen, killing his servants in the process. Fire falls from heaven and burns up his flocks and still more servants. Another tribe takes his camels. A house collapses and kills his sons and daughters.

Job tears his clothes and shaves his head in grief. Then he worships God and says, "Naked I came from my mother's womb, and naked I will depart. The LORD gave and the LORD has taken away; may the name of the LORD be praised" (Job 1:21 NIV).

Though he is devastated, he does not accuse God of wrongdoing.

The story continues. God remains proud of Job. Satan remains frustrated. During the next heavenly procession, God again points out his faithful servant Job. Satan gives the expected response: *Well, sure! You didn't let me strike Job's body. If I do, he'll curse you to your face.*

Most of us know the story. God gives permission. Satan strikes Job's flesh. Job ends up in such agony that he digs jagged pieces of pottery into his body in hopes of ending the pain.

It is at this point in the story that I start being impressed with the integrity of Job. For thirty-six chapters, which we are told may represent many weeks of suffering, Job endures criticism and self-satisfied advice from his wife and a handful of friends. Yet never, not once, does Job change his story. Not once does he admit what is not true. And never does he sin against God.

It is inspiring to behold. You see, there aren't very many conclusions to draw when something like this happens, when bad things happen to good people, and some of these few possible conclusions aren't very gratifying to consider. First, there is the possibility that God does not rule over all things after all. Perhaps the evil that befell Job just snuck by God. Second, there is the possibility God is not just. Maybe he answers righteousness with evil because he's, well, somewhat evil himself. Finally, there is also the possibility that human beings are actually innocent beings but that this does nothing to determine what happens to them.

Men were debating these matters in Job's day just as they were years later when his story was written down. They are still debating these things today.

The book of Job takes on the feel of a cosmic conflict examined through the experience of one man. Job's various friends are largely convinced Job is in sin or theological error. They make their case in windy sentences and flatulent self-confidence. Job stands his ground, and you love him for it. He says, essentially this: *Look, I'm not a perfect man, but there is no deep, dark sin in my life. If deserving has anything to do with what I've endured, I did not deserve this. I stand here in my integrity. I appeal to God. He knows the truth. I look to him to vindicate me.*

Keep in mind, the issue for Job is his integrity. His wife had taunted him with it: "Are you still maintaining your integrity?" (Job 2:9 NIV). The question stuck in his mind. Later, when his situation was at its worst, he told his friends, "I will never admit you are in the right; . . . I will not deny my integrity" (Job 27:5 NIV). A bit after that, when all seemed lost, he said simply, "Let him weigh me with honest scales; then God will discover my integrity" (Job 31:6 NET). Job wanted God to do exactly what the Roman centurions did to their men: test for integrity.

Job's running debate with his tiresome friends includes language that sounds the heart cry of all mankind. Imagine how many people have thought these words and how these sentences anticipate our hope for a savior: "[God] is not a man like me that I might answer him, that we might confront each other in court. If only there were

someone to arbitrate between us, to lay his hand upon us both, someone to remove God's rod from me, so that his terror would frighten me no more. Then I would speak up without fear of him, but as it now stands with me, I cannot" (Job 9:32–35 NIV).

We can feel one with Job's longing for God to act, his certainty that God knows the truth in all things: "If only I knew where to find him; if only I could go to his dwelling! I would state my case before him and fill my mouth with arguments. I would find out what he would answer me, and consider what he would say" (Job 23:3–5 NIV).

Finally, there is Job's hope, which echoes the hopes of millions of souls: "I know that my Redeemer lives, and that in the end he will stand upon the earth. And after my skin has been destroyed, yet in my flesh I will see God; I myself will see him with my own eyes—I, and not another. How my heart yearns within me!" (Job 19:25–27 NIV).

Despite these flashes of poetry and human longing, the book of Job drags severely. I think God wanted it to. The book is so long and so often tedious that you join Job in hoping God will intervene.

When he finally does, it is in one of the most magnificent displays of sovereignty you will ever have the privilege of witnessing. God breaks into the human wrangling and begins to speak. He does not explain himself. He does not soothe Job's feelings and pat him on the head. Nor does he enter into the human arguing or ever settle the matter of who was right.

Instead, he shows up with an attitude. *Shut up! Who are you to dare to speak? Did you speak the worlds into being? Did you set limits to the waves? Did you design the movement of a horse or the wonders of a woman's body? Then shut up! I am the Lord. I do as I please.*

God goes on like this for three chapters. Finally, Job repents and prays for God to forgive his idiot friends. Then God restores to Job nearly twice the prosperity he had before. And God leaves—having never explained himself.

You want to cheer at the end of the book of Job both because it is finally over and because God is so awe-inspiring and great. You don't know whether to shout like the home team just won the championship or to fall on your face and worship. Either way, it is a revelation.

What moves me deeply, aside from the unveiling of God's glory we all get to experience, is Job. He is in complete physical agony. He's lost everything. He has friends telling him what a fool and a sinner he is. Even his wife has turned against him. Still, he hopes for God and stands on what is true.

Job is a man! A manly man! I admire him. I've learned from him. Let me tell you what he has taught me:

1. Job will not be swayed by the opinions of men. He knows what is true. He listens respectfully to his friends. He is polite, yet he won't contort the truth to please a mere human. I wish I could say this has always been true of me. I hurt when men think ill of me. I find myself trying to win their favor. If I don't catch myself, I can start serving men for the paycheck of their approval and so find myself far from God and who I really am. No man can serve the opinions of other men and be his own man, a manly man. Job taught me this.

2. Job speaks the truth as he knows it. He understands the power of it. Whatever he has left in this life, he isn't going to lie. He stands on his integrity. He is willing to die from this experience if he must, but he is never going to say anything about it that isn't true. By contrast, I have often felt like a liar in a land of liars. The truth has sometimes seemed like an illusion to me, or perhaps like something too expensive to hold on to. Job whispered gently in my ear, "Truth is all you really have. Speak it in integrity. Be a man."

3. Job never accuses God. We are told this repeatedly in the forty-two chapters of the book: "In all this, Job did not sin by charging God with wrongdoing" (Job 1:22 NIV). We can see Job does not understand what is happening to him. He knows he has done nothing deserving the total destruction of all he holds dear. Yet he also knows God is just. Job might get angry. Job might curse his insulting friends. Job might regret his life in this world. But he never wavers from trust in God's character: "Though he slay me, yet will I hope in him" (Job 13:15 NIV). I've had some hard times, as most men have, but I've had nothing happen to me that approaches Job's suffering. Yet I cannot say I kept my faith in God as Job did. So Job helped me. The simple phrase, "Though he slay me, yet will I hope in him"—a reversal of everything this world lays upon us that it is—tells me what I need to know. God may do what he pleases, even if it means my destruction. Yet still, I keep my hope set on him. I say it again: Job was a man!

4. Job defends himself. He's not going to sit silently while lies are told and his character is assailed. He speaks. He gives an argument. He makes a defense. I've heard people say if a man defends himself vigorously he must be guilty. It's as though making a defense is itself a sin. I don't think so. I think it is the mark of righteousness in a person's soul. The apostle Paul thought so too. He told the church at Corinth they had obviously repented of their sins since they had an eagerness to clear themselves of wrongdoing (see 2 Corinthians 7:11). There is certainly a type of defensiveness and egotistical refusal to take correction that is ungodly and unproductive. A man needs to know the difference between this cowardly

behavior and the righteous desire to declare the truth. Job knew this difference. We should too.

5. Job was quick to admit his wrongs. Though he did not sin in accusing God, Job did have to admit that he "spoke of things I did not understand" (Job 42:3 NIV). This, too, is a sign of manly righteousness. Be teachable. Own your sins. Admit failings. Don't pretend to be what you are not. God alone is judge, and he already knows. This is a vital part of the truth to integrity. Be genuine, even if you were genuinely wrong and have to admit it to God and man.

6. Job listened to criticism. If what happened to Job had happened to me, the Book of Stephen would have been about three chapters long. I would not have sat around letting fools push their stupidity upon me. And I would never have come to the grand restoration that Job ultimately enjoyed. He seemed to know it is important to listen to your critics. One of the great arts of living is that you hear truth in the mouth of your enemies, that you let your critics be the unpaid guardians of your soul. It takes patience and a whole lot of self-control. Often, though, your critics can actually help you if you'll search, as a friend once said, for the diamonds of truth in the dunghill of men's opinions. I've learned this now—from Job.

7. Finally, Job waited. He might have killed himself. He might have cursed God. He might have killed his stunningly ignorant friends. He might have lost all hope. Instead, in agony and while a stench to his friends, he looked to God and waited. *I do not know what to do, but*

my eyes are on you. Men want to act, to fix what's wrong and broken. Sometimes, though, the better part of manhood is to know what you can't fix and to wait on the God who can. Waiting is hard. Waiting is a test. Waiting is also a way of saying, "God is God and I am not. He'll act when he's ready. Until then, I'm here." It may be the greatest statement of faith we can make, particularly during times of suffering. It's hard. That's why it's part of being a manly man.

WHAT THEN WILL YOU DO?
HOW WILL YOU SHOW YOURSELF A MAN?

1. Think carefully about your seasons of suffering. What do you see surfacing in your life at that time? Faith? Self-pity? Anger? Take note of it all. It is part of you. Turn it to prayer and ask God to make you a righteous man. Push back against your lesser self.

2. Hold your life against the seven lessons Job has taught us and see how you compare to this standard. Don't wait for some horrible, Joblike season of suffering to perfect these qualities. Put them into practice now. Ask those closest to you to tell you what they see when they hold you up against Job's Big Seven. Learn from them. Act.

3. Put yourself in intentional, short-term experiences of hardship. Train for something difficult, perhaps, or engage in spiritual disciplines like fasting and prolonged silence. Take note of what negative forces rise in your soul. Deal with them. Take note also of how you endure suffering, of what helps you get through it. Prayer? Scripture? A friend enduring at your side? The examples of great men of old? All of it is valid; strength comes differently for each of us. Know how it comes best for you.

4. Understand this principle well: if your theology—your view of the world based on God—doesn't include a biblical understanding of suffering, the hard things in life will surprise you and perhaps blow away your unprepared faith. Study your Bible on this topic. Talk to your band of brothers. Read good

books. Interview your spiritual mentors. Listen to the great men of old. Get biblical on the problem of evil and suffering in the world. Don't have such a lightweight religion that anything hard that befalls you knocks you from your foundation of faith. True men face hard things knowing who rules the world and knowing the good that hard things can produce. This is only true, though, if a man's theological worldview is big enough to include hard things in the first place.

"HE WHO LEARNS MUST SUFFER. AND EVEN IN OUR SLEEP, PAIN THAT CANNOT FORGET FALLS DROP BY DROP UPON THE HEART, AND IN OUR OWN DESPAIR, AGAINST OUR WILL, COMES WISDOM TO US BY THE AWFUL GRACE OF GOD."

—*Aeschylus, from the play* Agamemnon,
part of the trilogy Oresteia

A PSALM OF LIFE
WHAT THE HEART OF THE YOUNG MAN SAID TO THE PSALMIST

Tell me not, in mournful numbers,
Life is but an empty dream!
For the soul is dead that slumbers,
And things are not what they seem.

Life is real! Life is earnest!
And the grave is not its goal;
Dust thou art, to dust returnest,
Was not spoken of the soul.

Not enjoyment, and not sorrow,
Is our destined end or way;
But to act, that each to-morrow
Find us farther than today.

Art is long, and Time is fleeting,
And our hearts, though stout and brave,
Still, like muffled drums, are beating
Funeral marches to the grave.

In the world's broad field of battle,
In the bivouac of Life,
Be not like dumb, driven cattle!
Be a hero in the strife!

Trust no Future, howe'er pleasant!
Let the dead Past bury its dead!
Act,—act in the living Present!
Heart within, and God o'erhead!

Lives of great men all remind us
We can make our lives sublime,
And, departing, leave behind us
Footprints on the sands of time;

Footprints, that perhaps another,
Sailing o'er life's solemn main,
A forlorn and shipwrecked brother,
Seeing, shall take heart again.

Let us, then, be up and doing,
With a heart for any fate;
Still achieving, still pursuing,
Learn to labor and to wait.

—HENRY WADSWORTH LONGFELLOW

FORGIVENESS

He is among the greatest of Christian saints. His feast day is known well beyond the boundaries of the Christian church. With the possible exception of St. Nicholas, he is celebrated more lavishly than any other saint. Each March 17, parades, Celtic music, the wearing of green, and oceans of beer commemorate the memory of St. Patrick, the legendary apostle to Ireland. Though his life is largely unknown to us, what we do know tells us that Patrick was an awe-inspiring man.

He was also a man's man. He lived a rugged life, evangelized Ireland with beer and miracles, and eventually fought the raging enemy that comes for us all in the night. And he won. We'll come back to this.

The beer part of the story is fascinating. Patrick did not conduct Billy Graham-style crusades to evangelize the wild, pagan tribes of Ireland. Instead, he went tribe by tribe, chieftain by chieftain, building friendships and winning trust. Once he had that trust, he planted Christian communities among the tribes, and these in turn converted entire regions with holy living, miracles, generosity, healthy families, and prosperous farms. Beer also played a role.

Always at Patrick's side was his personal brewmaster, a man named Mescan. Patrick won many a chieftain by sharing the superior beer

Mescan had developed. When the chieftains saw this superior man named Patrick, took note of his superior way of living, and even tasted a superior quality in the beer Patrick offered them, it all seemed confirmation of the gospel Patrick preached. The Irish converted by the thousands.

Apparently, beer also played a role in some of the miracles Patrick performed. According to popular Irish legend, when the apostle once dined with the high king of Tara, "The wizard Lucatmael put a drop of poison into Patrick's cruse [an old English word for *pitcher*], and gave it into Patrick's hand: but Patrick blessed the cruse and inverted the vessel, and the poison fell thereout, and not even a little of the ale fell. And Patrick afterward drank the ale."[30]

We don't know with certainty if Patrick did all the great deeds legend records. Did his staff grow into a tree? Did he drive snakes out of Ireland? Did he use the shamrock to teach the Irish about the trinity? We simply can't be sure. We do know, though, that Patrick courageously strolled into violent pagan villages, befriended the chieftain, won both the man and the tribe with hospitality, served the needy, and by the end of his life had drawn most of Ireland to the gospel of Jesus Christ. What a life!

But this isn't all of it. How Patrick ended up in Ireland to spread Christianity in the first place—and the life he had lived in the years before—is just as interesting.

Patrick was born in Britain sometime late in the fourth century. His father was a Christian deacon, and his grandfather was a priest, but Patrick tells us in his *Confessio* that he had no faith of his own by the time he was sixteen. This is important to know because in that year of his life, pagan raiders kidnapped him and took him north to the Irish realms.

He spent the next six years as a captive and was made to tend herds on frigid pasturelands, ill fed and ill treated. It was a season of great suffering, but it served to return him to the Christianity of his fathers. We should hear this story in his own words:

> After I arrived in Ireland, I tended sheep every day, and I prayed frequently during the day. More and more the love of God increased, and my sense of awe before God. Faith grew, and my spirit was moved, so that in one day I would pray up to one hundred times, and at night perhaps the same. I even remained in the woods and on the mountain, and I would rise to pray before dawn in snow and ice and rain. I never felt the worse for it, and I never felt lazy—as I realise now, the spirit was burning in me at that time.[31]

During a season of fasting and prayer, Patrick heard a voice that said, "You do well to fast: soon you will depart for your home country." A short time later, another voice said, "Your ship is ready." Before long, deliverance did come, though the journey was arduous and it took several years for Patrick to make his way home. His parents were delighted by his return and also by his newly kindled faith. As loving parents would, they begged him to never travel far from them again.

Sometime later, Patrick began experiencing visions that turned his attention to the land where he had been a captive. Of one of these, Patrick later reported, "I saw a man whose name was Victoricus coming as if from Ireland with innumerable letters . . . and as I was reading the beginning of the letter I seemed at that moment to hear the voice of those who were beside the forest of Foclut which is near the western sea, and they were crying as if with one voice: 'We beg you, holy youth, that you shall come and shall walk again among us.'" After other similar visions, Patrick returned to the land of his captivity to spread the gospel of Christ.

It was an astonishing act. He had been cruelly abused during his six years among the Irish tribes. It could not have been easy to return. He surely battled fear and probably some bitterness, yet he courageously answered the call and, in time, shaped the course of history by his obedience.

What kind of man endures six years of cruel captivity and yet emerges with a new and vital faith? What kind of man returns to the land of his former captivity because he is touched by the needs of the people there? What kind of man converts warring pagan tribes with kindness, miracles, and beer? The answer is a holy man, an anointed man, a man who is chosen by God. Indeed, a true man, in the highest and grandest sense.

It would be natural to think that Patrick's greatest struggles were for the souls of the Irish people. We might easily expect that the church in Britain would be so thrilled at Patrick's evangelistic success and so eager to help that its leaders would do anything to keep from hindering the great man.

This didn't prove to be true.

Instead, the church in Britain allowed a storm of gossip and innuendo to undermine Patrick, distract him from his pioneering work, and threaten to damage him for the rest of his life. It was an agonizing time for this great apostle and it affords us an opportunity to watch him struggle as a man and emerge a greater man still.

He tells us in his *Confessio* that after he had already known great success among the Irish tribes, he learned he had been betrayed at home. It occurred during a season in which he was being considered for the office of a bishop. Elders who opposed this promotion began circulating rumors about him. This so wounded Patrick that he later wrote, "I was mightily upset, and might have fallen here and forever, but the Lord generously spared me, a convert, and an alien, for his name's sake, and he came powerfully to my assistance in that state of being trampled down."

I'll let Patrick tell the story himself, but since he speaks in sweeping, mystical phrases that are sometimes hard to understand, let me explain that this scandal had to do with a sin he'd confessed to a friend decades before. Apparently this friend told the church about Patrick's transgression to thwart his old friend's promotion to the episcopate, the office of bishop.

They brought up against me after thirty years an occurrence I had confessed before becoming a deacon. On account of the anxiety in my sorrowful mind, I laid before my close friend what I had perpetrated on a day—nay, rather in one hour—in my boyhood because I was not yet proof against sin. God knows—I do not—whether I was fifteen years old at the time, and I did not then believe in the living God, nor had I believed, since my infancy; but I remained in death and unbelief until I was severely rebuked, and in truth I was humbled every day by hunger and nakedness. . . .

Hence, therefore, I say boldly that my conscience is clear now and hereafter. God is my witness that I have not lied in these words to you.

But rather, I am grieved for my very close friend, that because of him we deserved to hear such a prophecy. The one to whom I entrusted my soul! And I found out from a goodly number of brethren, before the case was made in my defence (in which I did not take part, nor was I in Britain, nor was it pleaded by me), that in my absence he would fight in my behalf. Besides, he told me himself: "See, the rank of bishop goes to you"—of which I was not worthy. But how did it come to him, shortly afterwards, to disgrace me publicly, in the presence of all, good and bad, because previously, gladly and of his own free will, he pardoned me, as did the Lord, who is greater than all?

This is the type of assault many a man has endured, but in Patrick's case the stakes were high. He was already transforming the Irish realms with his message. Many new converts counted on his integrity. While engaged in his great work, an old friend betrayed Patrick's sin—a sin he had confessed thirty years before and which he committed when he was only fifteen and not yet a Christian.

We should pause Patrick's story here. He is fighting bitterness. He even admits that this bitterness might destroy him—forever. We should be thankful for his honesty. We have all fought this same merciless enemy—or we will.

For a man to become a great man, he will have to defeat the force of bitterness in his life. No one escapes it. There is enough offense and hardship in the world to assure that all of us will be wounded and betrayed, all of us will have opportunity to drink the sweet-tasting poison of bitterness against those who have wronged us. The art of surviving untainted is to learn the art of forgiveness.

It is a hard thing to do, and it seems to be harder for men. I'm making no excuses here. The majority of men seem to have souls coated with Velcro. Everything sticks, particularly every memory of a wrong, a hurt, a betrayal, or an offense. Men hold on to the wrongs done them, rehearse those wrongs, make excuses for failure out of those wrongs, and frequently poison their lives with the bitterness they keep circulating through their hearts and minds. It makes them small, blaming, angry souls rather than the large-hearted beings they are called to be. It damages everything they do and makes them wound those they are supposed to protect—wives, sons, daughters, and friends.

The keys to forgiveness are simple but costly, given our pride and self-pity. Someone wrongs us. It hurts. We work against our lesser nature and try to find the hook of compassion. John didn't hurt me because he hates me; he's feeling threatened. Or Jenny lashed out but

I should remember her background. Or those kids stole from me, but crime is all they know, all they've seen in the culture around them.

There are other reasons to forgive. We should cling to any of them that move us to do the right thing. It helps to remember we are sinners and have done a fair amount of damage ourselves. Frankly, it should scare us that God himself will not forgive those who do not forgive others. There is also the negative example of those who have made bitterness their life's work. Are they what we want to be? Small, angry, at war with life, at war with God, anchored to the past, and apart from the Holy Spirit?

No.

So we forgive. We send away the wrongs done to us. We let people out of the little cages we keep them in while we enjoy our feelings of moral superiority. We hand the feelings of wrong to God and refuse to ever take them back. Then we shut up and never mention the matter again. When the time comes, we put our arm around the offender and we ask him how he is. Usually a hearty meal together helps the process along, particularly if the offender is a he.

This is what it means to be clean of soul, to be a Christian, and to be a man. Anything less and it is the same as setting our manly hopes on fire and living with the ashes.

Before we return to Patrick, listen to this final thought from the eminent author Frederick Buechner:

> To lick your wounds, to smack your lips over grievances long past, to roll over your tongue the prospect of bitter confrontations still to come, to savor to the last toothsome morsel both the pain you are given and the pain you are giving back—in many ways it is a feast fit for a king. The chief drawback is that what you are wolfing down is yourself. The skeleton at the feast is you.[32]

It was not any easier for Patrick than it is for us, but he eventually did forgive. There are four words in his *Confessio* that tell us he drew the matter to an end and they are words that we ought to learn to use ourselves. After describing the whole affair of his betrayal, he wrote simply: "I have said enough." And he said no more. There might be a hint of the matter here or there in his writings, but they are vague: "I give untiring thanks to God who kept me faithful in the day of my temptation, so that today I may confidently offer my soul as a living sacrifice for Christ my Lord." This only helps us. Patrick had to fight, had to turn the whole matter to the Lord time and again. He knew, though, that the death of bitterness begins when we decide, "I have said enough." Thank God for Patrick's example.

WHAT THEN WILL YOU DO?
HOW WILL YOU SHOW YOURSELF A MAN?

1. Take a moment to evaluate your bitterness level. Don't trust yourself. Ask your wife, your older children, and your friends. Do they hear you rehearsing the wrongs you have suffered? Do they see you excusing yourself from God's will or from achievement with past wounds? Do they feel tainted by bitterness you spew?

2. Make a list of those you have not forgiven. Are you waiting for anyone to come to you and apologize? Then you haven't forgiven him. Have you chewed someone out—even when you're driving alone in your car!—for something he did to you? Then you haven't forgiven him. Do you feel pain when you think of your father, your mother, a coach, or a friend but then you say, inwardly or aloud, "I'm not going to go there"? If so, there is a failure to forgive. Be brutally honest. Ask those close enough to you to know. This is no time to spare yourself.

3. Get busy. Forgiveness is not a process of managing emotions. It is an act. You forgive. You tell people you forgive. You declare it done. You pray. You give the whole matter to God. You fight in prayer and rely on Scripture to strengthen you to stand free and clean. You ask people to forgive you. You do what you can to make amends. You get your life as free of bitter grudges and angry ways as possible. Finally, you ask the Holy Spirit to wash in afresh and to restore what has been lost during your poisoned season.

4. Remember your goal is not just an individual episode made clean. Your goal is to get the Velcro off of your soul and to replace it with righteous Teflon that won't let anything evil stick. So, you push in this direction. You ask God to work. You memorize scriptures that empower you in love. You realize offense is a cancer, and you deal with it as soon as it occurs. You fight. You declare war on your lesser nature. You get help from friends. You read books. You even watch movies that remind you of the damage bitterness does. There is no magic here. There is just a man fighting for his soul, using whatever he needs to be clean before God. In short, you act. It is what a man does.

"WE MUST DEVELOP AND MAINTAIN THE CAPACITY TO FORGIVE. HE WHO IS DEVOID OF THE POWER TO FORGIVE IS DEVOID OF THE POWER TO LOVE. THERE IS SOME GOOD IN THE WORST OF US AND SOME EVIL IN THE BEST OF US. WHEN WE DISCOVER THIS, WE ARE LESS PRONE TO HATE OUR ENEMIES."

—*Martin Luther King Jr., from "Loving Your Enemies," a sermon delivered at the Dexter Avenue Baptist Church in Montgomery, Alabama, Christmas 1957*

ANSWERING HIM

"When shall I be a man?" he said,
As I was putting him to bed.
"How many years will have to be
Before Time makes a man of me?
And will I be a man when I
Am grown up big?" I heaved a sigh,
Because it called for careful thought
To give the answer that he sought.

And so I sat him on my knee,
And said to him: "A man you'll be
When you have learned that honor brings
More joy than all the crowns of kings;
That it is better to be true
To all who know and trust in you
Than all the gold of earth to gain
If winning it shall leave a stain.

"When you can fight for victory sweet,
Yet bravely swallow down defeat,
And cling to hope and keep the right,
Nor use deceit instead of might;
When you are kind and brave and clean,
And fair to all and never mean;
When there is good in all you plan,
That day, my boy, you'll be a man."

—EDGAR A. GUEST

SUFFERING

Gentlemen, let me free you from a burden, the burden of the history you think you know.

We have all been done a great disservice. We have been taught what I call the statue version of history. By this I mean that we have been taught a version of history that presents the heroes of the past as moral giants who fell flawless from the womb, who achieved fame almost effortlessly. It hasn't served us well.

No one meant to do damage. Our history teachers probably thought they were simply honoring the great men and women of our past. Yet most of them gave us statues rather than human beings, unscarred giants who achieved and conquered as though there was never any question of their destiny.

It isn't so. Hear me. It is a lie.

The great heroes of the past you've grown to admire were all pitiful human beings whom we remember only because they declared war on some part of their pitifulness. If we don't know this, we are left to believe that some people are destined to be great but most of us aren't, and those of us who aren't should just settle down to our duties and shelve whatever dreams make our hearts race.

I'll say it again. It's a lie.

God sets destinies in heaven, but those destinies have to be hammered out on earth one arduous minute at a time. We strain. We bleed. We grieve. We have to conquer each step. No one gets a pass. No one moves to the head of the line, even if he gets a statue. Everyone is flawed.

Listen. John Wesley was a great man. He founded the Methodist church and helped lead England in a transformative spiritual renewal. He was a great man.

Yet his marriage was so bad that when a friend went to pick him up for a meeting, the man found Wesley's wife dragging the great preacher around the house by the hair. The woman pretty much despised her husband. Sometimes she went to his preaching meetings—to heckle him! I'm not exaggerating a bit when I tell you that Methodist and non-Methodist historians alike have concluded that one of the reasons John Wesley rode tens of thousands of miles to preach the gospel throughout the British Isles was that he didn't want to go home.

Here's another example. Try to figure out who this next man is: He was a great man. One of the greatest. And yet, he was in debt every day of his adult life. His marriage was often troubled. One of his children committed suicide. He once made a decision that threw his entire country into economic turmoil. He was, for a long period, the most hated political figure in his nation. Even when he was the leader of that nation, he refused to spend the night in a room with a balcony. Why? Because he suffered from horrible bouts of depression and he never knew when another episode might strike. He feared that one day the darkness would come for him and he would try to jump to his death.

Quite a tormented person, right? You wouldn't want this man mowing your yard—you don't want a suicidal guy with a lawnmower around your house! But I'm talking about Winston Churchill, the greatest leader of the twentieth century.

Why don't we teach important details like this—the whole truth about great leaders—in our schools? Wouldn't it help kids with problems—which is to say, all of them—understand that they can achieve, too; that they aren't irreparable misfits because they have a few challenges?

Churchill wasn't alone. One of the greatest men in American history, Abraham Lincoln, also fought depression and was also suicidal upon occasion, at least in the first half of his life. It didn't change the fact that Abraham Lincoln was a great man, perhaps the greatest of our presidents.

His best friend said he dripped melancholy as he walked. Another close friend said Lincoln had the saddest face he ever saw. Lincoln once wrote, "I am now the most miserable man living. If what I feel were equally distributed to the whole human family, there would not be one cheerful face on the earth. Whether I shall ever be better I cannot tell; I awfully forbode I shall not."[33]

Grief haunted him all his days. A younger brother died when he was a small child. His mother died when he was nine. Abe helped his father make the casket and lower her body in the ground. His sister died when he was sixteen, and the first—and, some historians suspect, the only—woman he ever loved died young too. He buried two sons and as president felt the deaths of hundreds of thousands in the war he could not prevent nor bring quickly to a close.

He was haunted all his life by the thought of rain falling on graves.

He was not merely sad from time to time. He was chronically, manically depressed. He called it "the hypo." It was short for *hypochondriasis*, the term in his day for a number of syndromes, including depression. His friend Joshua Speed said that Lincoln once "went Crazy as a Loon." Friends had to "remove razors from his room—take away all Knives and other such dangerous things—it was terrible."[34]

Lincoln considered suicide so often he even wrote a poem about it. Just a few verses reveal the darkness that tormented his soul.

Here, where the lonely hooting owl
Sends forth his midnight moans,
Fierce wolves shall o'er my carcass growl,
Or buzzards pick my bones. . . .

Yes! I've resolved the deed to do,
And this place to do it:
This heart I'll rush a dagger through
Though I in hell should rue it!

Sweet steel! Come forth from out of your sheath,
And glist'ning, speak your powers;
Rip up the organs of my breath,
And draw my blood in showers.

I strike! It quivers in that heart
Which drives me to this end;
I draw and kiss the bloody dart,
My last—my only friend![35]

Keep in mind that Lincoln was a lawyer and a member of the Illinois state legislature at the time.

His sadness often spilled over despite himself. He once wrote these words to a young girl he knew.

To Rosa—
You are young, and I am older;
You are hopeful, I am not—

Enjoy life, ere it grows colder—
Pluck the roses ere they rot.[36]

The child had merely asked Lincoln to sign her autograph book. He couldn't stop himself. He was engulfed in misery.

Yet Lincoln did not surrender to this darkness. He changed. He grew. He deepened in faith and learned to silence the voices of death that came to him in the night. He overcame, and later helped the nation do the same.

What we most need to know about Lincoln's battle with depression is it helped to make him a better man—not the depression itself, but rather what was produced in Lincoln as he fought back against the depression.

He learned to master his thoughts. It helped to give him a disciplined mind. He learned to reach for tactics to dispel his gloom. It helped to give him his famous sense of humor. His depression forced him to view life almost as an outsider. This gave him perspective and graced him with the poetic sense we hear in his magnificent speeches.

More than one historian has made the point that as agonizing as Lincoln's struggle with depression was for him, it nevertheless gave us the Lincoln we know.

This is one of the great truths of life. Great men suffer greatly in order to be great. Heroic men must first endure heroic struggles with themselves. I've never read about a great man or woman of whom this was not true.

This is about more than Lincoln, though. It is about you and all the men you know. We know our flaws—at least most of them. We constantly

face our weaknesses and our damage. It can cause us to doubt we will ever live an exceptional life. It isn't true. If history is any guide, struggling manfully against our deformities is the beginning of greatness.

I believe most men make peace with their defects. They accept their flaws as simply the way they are, and so they never declare war on those parts of themselves that keep them from exceptional lives. Mediocrity becomes their lot in life; merely getting by their only hope.

The question we all face is not whether or not we have defects. We do. Every one of us. The question is whether we are capable of envisioning a life defined by forces greater than the weight of our flaws. The moment we can—the moment we can envision a life beyond mere compromise with our deformities—that is the moment we take the first steps toward weighty lives.

Manly men know themselves, work to understand their God-ordained uniqueness and their unique brand of damage, and accept they will always be a work in progress, always be a one-man construction project that is never quite finished in this life. They don't despair. They don't settle. They don't expect perfection of themselves. They understand that destiny is in the hand of God. They also understand that these destinies are fashioned in a man's struggle against the enemies of his soul.

WHAT THEN WILL YOU DO?
HOW WILL YOU SHOW YOURSELF A MAN?

1. Take inventory of the unique flaws and deformities in your life. Have the courage to ask those closest to you what they think these defects might be.
2. Go to the root of these issues. What has caused them? Wounds? Conditioning? Wrong beliefs? Flawed religion?
3. In counsel with friends and pastors, make an action plan. Declare war on your weaknesses and the imperfections in your life. Most of us have too many defects to attack all at one time, but by identifying the ones that most undermine your progress toward being a genuine man, you will have established the target of your battle plan.
4. Warning: We can become preoccupied with ourselves through a process like this. In a noble effort to improve with God's help, we can spend far too much time thinking about ourselves and end up building a bigger and more disqualifying stronghold of self than we started with. Stay focused. Identify the enemies of your soul. Develop a strategy against them. Understand you have begun a lifelong process. Get on with living, aware of your flaws. This is a means of mastering yourself, not a process by which to become even more self-focused. Enough said.
5. Finally, remember wounds and deformities draw us inward. Overcoming them frees us to focus on others and love them as God intends. The measure of your progress is the increase of your investment in the lives entrusted to you. As Lincoln

overcame his depression, he became a bigger soul, a grander visionary, a man more in love with his nation, and, ultimately, a more effective servant to his people. This is exactly why a man's battle to overcome himself is often the same thing as his battle to fulfill his destiny.

> ## "I HAVE MISSED MORE THAN 9,000 SHOTS IN MY CAREER. I HAVE LOST ALMOST 300 GAMES. ON 26 OCCASIONS I HAVE BEEN ENTRUSTED TO TAKE THE GAME WINNING SHOT . . . AND I MISSED. I HAVE FAILED OVER AND OVER AND OVER AGAIN IN MY LIFE. AND THAT'S PRECISELY WHY I SUCCEED."
>
> —*Michael Jordan, from* The Sign of the Swoosh *by Robert Goldman and Stephen Papson (1998)*

HOW DID YOU DIE?

Did you tackle that trouble that came your way
With a resolute heart and cheerful?
Or hide your face from the light of day
With a craven soul and fearful?
Oh, a trouble's a ton, or a trouble's an ounce,
Or a trouble is what you make it,
And it isn't the fact that you're hurt that counts,
But only how did you take it?

You are beaten to earth? Well, well, what's that?
Come up with a smiling face.
It's nothing against you to fall down flat,
But to lie there—that's disgrace.
The harder you're thrown, why the higher you bounce;
Be proud of your blackened eye!
It isn't the fact that you're licked that counts,
It's how did you fight—and why?

And though you be done to the death, what then?
If you battled the best you could,
If you played your part in the world of men,
Why, the Critic will call it good.
Death comes with a crawl, or comes with a pounce,
And whether he's slow or spry,
It isn't the fact that you're dead that counts,
But only how did you die?

—EDWARD VANCE COOKE

VISION

SOME MEN SEEM TO BE TOUGH AND AGGRESSIVE FROM BIRTH. They take naturally to a life of rough play and muscular, adventurous living. Other men seem nearly the opposite. They find their rowdier friends tiresome and prefer more refined, delicate ways.

There are also men who have every reason to live prim, restricted lives given their body types, the nature of their gifts, perhaps their deformities, and even, in some cases, the injustices done to them. Yet some men in this latter category have such inner toughness, possess such a manliness of soul, and are captured by such a brilliant vision of heroic manhood that they are able to defy their bodies and their conditioning in order to reach for a masculine life by sheer force of will.

This was Rudyard Kipling, and, though study of his life and writings has fallen out of fashion today, he was a manly man who knew what genuine manhood was and used his skill with words to define it for his generation. Today it is virtually impossible to discuss manly ways without referring to his magnificent poem, "If—." It is the defining poetic statement of the manly virtues.

Yet this brilliant articulation of vital manhood came from the pen of a small, unathletic, bespectacled, bookish, bullied, insecure man whom friends expected would become almost anything other than

the prophet of manhood for his time. How we need men like him today—men who refuse to let biology define their destiny and who live inspired by a fiery inner vision of the masculine life.

The truth is that Rudyard Kipling's body of work may have slowed the decline of western manhood, keeping it from falling into the dust decades before its recent troubled season. His writings—poems, essays, and fiction for both adults and children—filled the last decades of the nineteenth century and the opening decades of the twentieth with chest-thumping bravado, unabashed patriotism, full-throated praise of valor, and the glorification of manly adventure. Men the world over heard his words as a trumpet call. It is a call that echoes even now, nearly eight decades after the poet laureate of manly men passed from this life.

His grandfathers on both sides were Wesleyan ministers. He was born in Bombay, the son of a British teacher and his exceptionally gifted wife. His first five years of life in that boisterous city stirred Kipling's imagination and inspired him to speak of his mother with affection all his days. Everything changed for him in 1871, though—the year his parents followed the custom of the day and left him in England with his sister to attend school. For the six years that followed, brother and sister were brutalized in the harsh, legalistic, unsympathetic care of a woman named Holloway who lived in the south of England. As we might expect, Kipling tells the story best:

> Then came a new small house smelling of aridity and emptiness, and a parting in the dawn with Father and Mother, who said that I must learn quickly to read and write so that they might send me letters and books.
>
> I lived in that house for close on six years. It belonged to a woman

who took in children whose parents were in India. She was married to an old Navy Captain . . . Then the old Captain died, and I was sorry, for he was the only person in that house as far as I can remember who ever threw me a kind word.

It was an establishment run with the full vigour of the Evangelical as revealed to the Woman. I had never heard of Hell, so I was introduced to it in all its terrors . . . Myself I was regularly beaten. The Woman had an only son of twelve or thirteen as religious as she. I was a real joy to him, for when his mother had finished with me for the day he (we slept in the same room) took me on and roasted the other side.

If you cross-examine a child of seven or eight on his day's doings (specially when he wants to go to sleep) he will contradict himself very satisfactorily.

If each contradiction be set down as a lie and retailed at breakfast, life is not easy. I have known a certain amount of bullying, but this was calculated torture—religious as well as scientific. Yet it made me give attention to the lies I soon found it necessary to tell: and this, I presume, is the foundation of literary effort.[37]

Mrs. Kipling returned to England in 1877 and removed the children from Holloway's care. Later, she learned of her son's brutal treatment and wondered why he never asked for help. As he explained in the years after, "Children tell little more than animals, for what comes to them they accept as eternally established. Also, badly-treated children have a clear notion of what they are likely to get if they betray the secrets of a prison-house before they are clear of it."[38]

In 1878, Rudyard entered the United Services College at Westward Ho!, Devon, a school designed to prepare British boys for the army. Again, he suffered under the hostile rule of bullies. His poor eyesight, slight frame, lack of athletic skill, and inherent bookishness made him an obvious target.

My first year and a half was not pleasant. The most persistent bullying came not less from the bigger boys, who merely kick and pass on,
than from the young devils of fourteen acting in concert against one
butt. . . . I played footer [rugby] but here again my sight hampered
me. I was not even in the Second Fifteen.

After my strength came suddenly to me about my fourteenth
year, there was no more bullying; and either my natural sloth or past
experience did not tempt me to bully in my turn.[39]

Graduation in 1882 moved him to take honest stock of his life. He
determined he did not have the academic strength to attend Oxford
University and he had long accepted he would never have a successful
military career. He decided to accept a job his father secured for him:
assistant editor of the *Civil and Military Gazette* in Lahore, India
(now Pakistan).

So, at sixteen years and nine months, but looking four or five years
older, and adorned with real whiskers which the scandalized Mother
abolished within one hour of beholding, I found myself at Bombay
where I was born, moving among sights and smells that made me
deliver in the vernacular sentences whose meaning I knew not. . . .
There were yet three or four days' rail to Lahore, where my people
lived. After these, my English years fell away, nor ever, I think, came
back in full strength.[40]

Typical of men who are destined for influence and power, his failures and setbacks served him well. His English education, his love of
India, his talent for the written word, and his poetic sense all converged
as he took a job with an obscure newspaper in British India. An Oxford
education might have denuded his literary gifts, and a military life
might have hardened him beyond repair. In later years he was grateful

to have escaped both. Yet to be in India, writing, reclaiming the imagination of his youth, and observing the ways of men with a journalist's eye—this was the making of poet and storyteller Rudyard Kipling.

He acquired a ruggedness of soul that began to reveal itself in his writing. He was courageous—but in print, seldom having stepped onto a contested battlefield. He was principled—but with a pen, not in his nation's halls of power. He was fierce—but in the pursuit of a manly vision, not in the pursuit of the empire's enemies. He wrote of the thrashing Indian frontier with love for the ways of men and devotion to the ideals of English manhood, but he was always the observer, seldom the participant.

Still, he played his role. He mastered an artillery of words he used to expose the foppish ways and low morals that had become fashionable among men of his time. He first wrote articles and a column for the *Gazette*. On the side, he experimented with short stories. In a display of the industriousness that would mark his career, in 1888 he published six collections of short stories, proving him a master of the art. It was an astonishing output for a beginning author. Soon after, he left India to tour America—where he met Mark Twain—and then returned to England in 1889.

He continued to write at an astonishing pace, but it became too much for him and he suffered a nervous breakdown. Doctors prescribed a journey by sea and this took him to Australia, South Africa, and New Zealand before allowing him to visit India once again. He married in 1892 and settled with his new wife in Vermont. He would live alternatively in the United States, in England, and, for brief seasons, in South Africa for the rest of his life.

Marriage settled him and made him a more deliberate, more thoughtful writer. The four decades from his wedding to his death, from 1892 to 1936, was a time of magnificent literary output that eventually earned him the Nobel Prize in literature. He wrote enduring classics like

The Jungle Book, Captains Courageous, Just So Stories, The Light That Failed, and *Kim.* His poetry, which dealt with themes of empire, heroism, and the conflict of cultures, included "Gunga Din," "Recessional," "The White Man's Burden," and, of course, the magnificent "If—."

Kipling understood the necessity of brutal force in the service of righteousness, but he also understood the tragedy of war and the flaws of fallen men. His poetry captured both, and proved capable of touching his readers with the capacity of human virtue and also with the sadness of loss and decline.

His legacy was fashioned not only by his ability to sound the genuine tones of the human—and, more specifically, the masculine—experience, but also by his nearly inhuman capacity to work. A contemporary, William James Dawson, wrote in a work entitled *The Making of Manhood,* "Rudyard Kipling owes everything to work. He has led one of the hardest and most strenuous lives. Of course, he has genius, imaginative power, observation; but they have been trained and developed in the school of hard work . . . Depend upon it, behind all great achievement there lies great toil: nothing that is worth doing is done easily."[41]

Kipling's words transcended his time and helped to frame the meaning of manhood for the generations that followed him. Consider these two stanzas from "The Young British Soldier":

If your officer's dead and the sergeants look white,
Remember it's ruin to run from a fight:
So take open order, lie down, and sit tight,
And wait for supports like a soldier.
Wait, wait, wait like a soldier . . .

When you're wounded and left on Afghanistan's plains,
And the women come out to cut up what remains,
Jest roll to your rifle and blow out your brains

An' go to your Gawd like a soldier.
Go, go, go like a soldier,
Go, go, go like a soldier,
Go, go, go like a soldier,
Soldier of the Queen!

The words are typical of Kipling's ideals, his vision of manhood and the nobility of the empire. Yet he could also pen sentences of stark realism and grief: "There be certain times in a young man's life, when, through great sorrow or sin, all the boy in him is burnt and seared away so that he passes at one step to the more sorrowful state of manhood."[42]

Always, there appeared in his writing a manly sense of honor for the gifts of the fathers. In his poem "The Old Issue" he wrote:

All we have of freedom
All we use or know
This our fathers bought for us
Long and long ago.

What Rudyard Kipling teaches us, among so much else, is that rugged, courageous manhood is not exclusively a matter of strength and speed, of physical skill and athletic prowess. It is first a condition of soul: a vision of what masculinity is and can be.

Knowing this frees us from a trite brand of manhood that is only about the life of the body and the physical world. Instead, it teaches us that genuine manhood grows from a man's inner life. It is born of a sense of responsibility and oriented to virtues that have the power to distinguish the life of a man from every other kind of life on earth.

From this, every masculine duty and discipline grows, and no one put this into words like the rather unlikely figure of Rudyard Kipling. He gave us language for describing and encouraging the masculine life in ourselves, in our sons, in the men of our generation. In doing so he also painted the vision that has inspired men the world over toward genuine manhood. He was a small, bookish, bespectacled man whom no one thought of as physically masculine. Yet he proved to be one of the most masculine of men in the only way that is ultimately important: in the manliness of the vision that guided his life and set his message aflame.

WHAT THEN WILL YOU DO?
HOW WILL YOU SHOW YOURSELF A MAN?

1. Make sure you have not mistaken physical bravado and an animal type of aggression for manhood. While genuine manhood is about action, it is not merely about a man's physical life. Make sure you are clear about the difference and are not imbalanced.

2. Take Kipling's poem "If—" and work through it slowly with friends. Apply each principle to your life. Where are you satisfied with how you are living out the words of this poem? Where do its words convict you? Don't be afraid to use it as a checklist of manly ethics.

3. How are you ensuring that your version of manliness is not merely an act but that it grows from a rugged soul, a principled vision, and an inner devotion to the manly virtues? How are you staying inspired to live as a manly man? What are you reading, watching, memorizing, and applying that will make you an exceptional man? If you find yourself lacking in this area, use some of the resources at the back of this book to fashion an "upgrade program" for yourself and, as always, enlist the encouragement and mentoring of friends.

"THE BRAVEST ARE SURELY THOSE WHO HAVE
THE CLEAREST VISION OF WHAT IS BEFORE
THEM, GLORY AND DANGER ALIKE, AND YET
NOTWITHSTANDING, GO OUT TO MEET IT."

—*Thucydides, from* History of the Peloponnesian War, Book II

IF—

If you can keep your head when all about you
Are losing theirs and blaming it on you,
If you can trust yourself when all men doubt you,
But make allowance for their doubting too;
If you can wait and not be tired by waiting,
Or being lied about, don't deal in lies,
Or being hated, don't give way to hating,
And yet don't look too good, nor talk too wise:
If you can dream—and not make dreams your master;
If you can think—and not make thoughts your aim;
If you can meet with Triumph and Disaster
And treat those two impostors just the same;
If you can bear to hear the truth you've spoken
Twisted by knaves to make a trap for fools,
Or watch the things you gave your life to, broken,
And stoop and build 'em up with worn-out tools:
If you can make one heap of all your winnings
And risk it on one turn of pitch-and-toss,
And lose, and start again at your beginnings
And never breathe a word about your loss;
If you can force your heart and nerve and sinew
To serve your turn long after they are gone,
And so hold on when there is nothing in you
Except the Will which says to them: "Hold on!"

If you can talk with crowds and keep your virtue,
Or walk with Kings—nor lose the common touch,
If neither foes nor loving friends can hurt you,
If all men count with you, but none too much;
If you can fill the unforgiving minute
With sixty seconds' worth of distance run,
Yours is the Earth and everything that's in it,
And—which is more—you'll be a Man, my son!

—RUDYARD KIPLING

HUMILITY

IT IS OFTEN SAID THAT MEN ARE EMBARRASSED BY THEIR EMO-
tions, that they find feelings complex and messy. There is some truth
to this—for some men, some of the time. The truth, though, is that
for most men emotions simply aren't primary. Men feel, but their feelings don't usually come first for them. They have emotions, but their
emotions come after other factors in importance. This doesn't make
them heartless. It also doesn't mean they lack healthy emotions. And
it certainly doesn't mean their sometimes stoic ways make them better than women, or better than other men whose feelings are more at
the surface.

This does explain, though, why much of Christianity, and much of
what society wants men to do, can seem to them like a game of "emotion management." It may also explain why we are losing men from the
church and from frontline roles nationwide.

We would look at this dynamic carefully. It is the reason most
men's ministries, therapy groups, retreats, books, and even small
groups fail. Someone somewhere wants men to feel something different and then act differently. They want men to manage their emotions
as the path to managing their behavior.

It probably won't happen. And it doesn't have to.

Here's why: men are more likely to feel *after* doing than they are to feel their way *to* doing. It's how they are made. It's fine, really. In fact, this order of feelings in relation to action can be a far more productive arrangement than the other way around.

Let's look at an example. Consider the issue of forgiveness. In most churches and therapy groups, men are taught that forgiving is largely about feeling differently toward someone who has offended. We must kneel, ask God to forgive us for being such hard-hearted beings, and determine instantly to have different thoughts and emotions regarding a person who has wronged us. I believe this makes a demand that is both unwise and unbiblical. It may be the reason that many people find it so difficult to forgive and instead end up holding on to offenses their whole lives.

The truth is that forgiving is more about doing than feeling. Forgiving is primarily a decision to treat a wrong in the same way we cancel the debt of someone who owes us money. We no longer hold the debtor in a debtor's prison. We forgive the debt by deciding we are no longer owed anything: an apology, an opportunity to beat the offender to death, the right to talk nasty about him or her. Instead, we *decide*—not feel—the record is wiped clean. We refuse to speak ill of the one who has harmed us. Instead, we act kindly toward them. We speak positive words, change behavior, refuse to make excuses, even go to the offender/debtor and *do* whatever reconciliation and restored friendship demands.

Forgiveness is about doing. It is far more than wrestling emotions in secret. We act. And, in time, the feelings come. It rarely works the other way around.

I have a friend who is a dynamic leader and a fiery Christian. He takes the command to "bless your enemy" seriously. If he reads something negative about himself in the paper or if he hears that somebody has spoken ill of him, he'll say out loud to several of us, "No, he shouldn't do that! I'm gonna have to bless him. See? See what this dude is makin' me do? I'm gonna have to pour some good on his boney backside and love on him. Here it comes. Oh no! He's not ready for this."

My friend then writes a check to the pastor who spoke ill of him, or does something kind for the reporter who told lies about him. Let me tell you what happens then. My friend gets bigger in spirit. Most of the people who thought they didn't like him end up becoming his friends. But no one sits around waiting for feelings to land. They just act. All the feelings come, but later, after the doing is done. And usually the winner is the kingdom of God. It's amazing to see.

This same truth applies to men and humility. The most important aspect of being humble isn't that we feel a certain set of emotions. The most important matter is that we humble ourselves—do deeds of humility—as a lifestyle, trusting that genuine humility will come from the "outside in" as the Holy Spirit honors our obedience.

So this is what striving for humility looks like in my life. I defer to other men. I submit to my elders. I try not to praise myself to others. I fail. I repent. I confess. I fast, in part, to live fully aware of my own weakness. I open my heart to rebuke when friends and leaders see something amiss in my life. I also submit to my wife, not only because the apostle Paul urged mutual submission of husbands and wives in his letter to the Ephesians, but also because I recognize her superior gifts. I try to see myself as small in my own eyes. I give up certain rights. All these things I do in pursuit of humility no matter how I feel at the time. Frankly, I do not often "feel humble." I have, though, been making progress in humility by humbling myself—that is, doing deeds of humility.

This approach gets closer to the heart of a man. He is made to *do* first. Feelings come later—if at all. And thank God for it. Where would we be if the men who have shaped our world waited to feel before they acted?

Certainly, a man who is whole is able to feel and he should hope to have a rich emotional life. Yet a man who is whole also does not regard feelings as a mandate for action. He acts as a mandate for feeling.

Few men have modeled the deeds of humility quite like the man in the story I'm about to tell you. During the first decade of the last century, an older woman decided to sit for a moment in the lobby of an elegant Des Moines hotel. She was weary and parched. She turned to a slender, well-dressed black man who was standing nearby and asked him to fetch a glass of water for her. The man immediately went to the front desk of the hotel and returned with the water. Handing it to the woman, he asked, "Ma'am, is there anything else I can get for you?" The woman said there wasn't and the man walked off.

I know this doesn't sound like that important a story. What I have not told you is that the man was, at that time, the most famous black man in the world. He was the president of a prestigious institute. He had once dined with the president of the United States. He was an advisor to kings and prime ministers and he was an internationally renowned author. Yet when a tired woman mistook him for a waiter because of the color of his skin, he took no offense. He did what she asked, and then he offered to do more. It was an extraordinarily humble act, but it was typical of this man. His name was Booker T. Washington, and the humility he displayed that day was just the brand of humility he had been urging upon his people and his nation for years.

It was Theodore Roosevelt who had invited Booker T. Washington to dine in the White House. Afterward, Roosevelt wrote:

To a very extraordinary degree, he combined humility and dignity; and I think that the explanation of his extraordinary degree of success in a very difficult combination was due to the fact that at the

bottom of his humility was really the outward expression, not of a servile attitude toward any man, but of the spiritual fact that in very truth he walked humbly with his God.[44]

Booker T. Washington's gracious act in that Des Moines hotel lobby flowed naturally from the course of his life. He was born to a slave woman on a Virginia farm in 1856. A census taken a few years later listed him as "1 Negro Boy (Booker)–$400." He lived through the horrors of the Civil War with his mother, Jane, and at war's end moved with her to Malden, West Virginia. It was there he became an employee of Viola Ruffner, a demanding New England schoolteacher who gave him his first lessons in responsibility. In later years, he attributed much of what he became to her influence.

He attended Hampton Normal School, a unique institution built on the idea that the greatest need of freed slaves was character, not charity. It was not a message most African Americans embraced at the time. Booker absorbed this philosophy into his core, graduated from Hampton as a star student, and, after teaching there for a season, moved to Alabama to open a newly chartered school with the name Tuskegee Normal and Industrial Institute.

The school became the vehicle for Booker's bold, controversial philosophy. He believed character, cleanliness, industriousness, skill, godliness, and patience would mean advancement for black America. If blacks made themselves valuable to whites, equality would come. Guided by this promise, Washington designed Tuskegee to teach trades from brickmaking to typing, restore the priority of character, and imprint the values of Christianity upon the souls of his students.

He believed unearned wealth would harm his race and leave them forever an underclass. He was certain that "habits of thrift, a love of work, economy, ownership of property, bank accounts" would lead to his people's ascent. It was the message he preached to the nation and the guiding principle of his work at Tuskegee.

Many blacks, like Harvard scholar W. E. B. DuBois, disagreed. They felt keenly the wrongs done to them by white society and looked to political processes and social aid as the sources of black advancement. They trusted in laws more than markets, in courts more than the kindly intentions of white America.

At the heart of Booker T. Washington's vision for blacks was confidence in the power of humility. He agreed with William Mountford, who wrote, "It is from out of the depths of our humility that the height of our destiny looks grandest."[45] Washington was no coward and did not think humility the best posture of his people because he feared another course. Instead, he believed humility won the favor of God, caused a man to live simply and genuinely rather than merely to impress, and freed him from vanity so he could know himself and know the world as it was, rather than as he wished it to be.

Washington knew the temptation of the freed slave. Having been subjugated for so long, it was natural for a man just liberated from his chains to live for pleasure, excess, and a resentful type of ostentation. Booker T. Washington taught that ex-slaves who lived like this merely fashioned new chains for themselves—chains of the soul and the spirit, chains of debt and materialism. He believed he had been sent as something of a prophet to urge his people toward a higher path.

History may conclude that he was wrong about many things. He certainly overestimated the kind intentions of white society. Some whites hate blacks just for their skin color, no matter how gifted and productive and polite those blacks might be. This truth, dawning upon Booker late in life, was a heartbreaking tragedy for him.

Yet he was certainly right about the value of humility in a man's life. In this he was prophet to men and women of all races and colors. That he died in 1915—just as the United States was stepping into a bloody European war and a movie entitled *The Birth of a Nation* portrayed blacks as criminals and the Ku Klux Klan as liberators (and was shown in Woodrow Wilson's White House!)—signaled how urgently the dawning century would need Booker T. Washington's message. It was an age with no ear to hear, though, and so it became the bloodiest, most tragic century in history. Yet, there—before it all began—was Booker T. Washington, urging simple lives, productive lives, righteous lives, each permeated by the humility Mr. Washington had shown in that Des Moines hotel.

Booker T. Washington has much to teach us as men. The powerful force of humility is certainly the greatest among them. His brand of humility was, as President Roosevelt had said of him, not the fruit of fear or insecurity. It came, instead, from a yearning to know the world in truth and to live a genuine life, freed from blinding vanity, impoverishing materialism, and burdensome debt.

Yet Mr. Washington also taught that *doing* humility is the path to being humble. Do humble deeds, he taught, and a humble heart will follow. This is good news for modern men striving to be manly men. Character is not out of our reach. It is not a lifelong battle to organize our emotions. Instead, it is a decision to act and to act consistently, knowing that emotions are usually a result and not a cause.

How liberating this is. A man can say to his son as men can say to each other, "Go be humble," and the words require no need to manage feelings. Just do what is right; do what is humble. God will see and work in you to see his will complete.

Act, my friends. *Do*. It is the way of men.

WHAT THEN WILL YOU DO?
HOW WILL YOU SHOW YOURSELF A MAN?

1. Take note of the areas of your life in which you've been trying to perfect virtue by managing your emotions rather than by acting, by doing something that needs to be done. How has this hindered you? What actions can you take to begin *doing* humility that you hadn't thought of before?

2. List practical ways in which you can humble yourself and have friends hold you accountable for actually doing them. At the same time, memorize the scriptures that promise the Holy Spirit will produce the fruit of humility in your life. True humility will come from your offering of obedience and the Holy Spirit's faithfulness to work in you. Hold to this confidence, pray for it often, and *act.*

3. Is there any area of your life where you have done damage through haughtiness and pride? Of course, we all do damage through pride through the years, but is there an ongoing area like this in your life now? Go after it. Address it. Apologize. Repent. Confess. Call your band of brothers in to help.

4. Finally, don't ignore healthy emotions. I urge action over emotion in this book, but I also urge that emotions are important in their right priority. Don't ignore the importance of a healthy soul and healthy emotions. I suggest you pray Psalm 23:3 every day. *Lord, please be my good shepherd and restore my soul.* If you do this, you will be enlisting God's help in healing any emotional damage you have sustained and in restoring you to what you are made to be.

"I FIND MORE AND MORE THAT TRUE
HUMILITY CONSISTS IN BEING SUBMISSIVE
TO THOSE WHO ARE A LITTLE ABOVE OR
A LITTLE BELOW US. OH, WHEN SHALL I
COME TO REJOICE IN OTHERS' GIFTS AND
GRACES AS MUCH AS IN MY OWN!"

—*George Whitefield, from* Sketches of the life and
labours of the Rev George Whitefield *(1850)*

SACRIFICE

We have come far enough in this exploration of manhood for you to form one of the most important conclusions about your life as a man. You are called to sacrifice. There just isn't a way to say it any more clearly. Genuine manhood, manly manhood, true manhood—is sacrifice. To do manly things, tend your field, make manly men, and live to the glory of God—in other words, to fulfill all the Manly Maxims—you have to sacrifice.

Sacrifice what? Everything. Anything. Not your integrity or morality or commitments to God, but certainly your comforts, your rights, your time, your money, your attention, and your energy. You have to sacrifice the priority of yourself.

I've tried in this book to use the example of men in history rather than the statements of Scripture, simply because I want you to experience manhood by example rather than by precept. Yet consider the power of something the apostle Paul said. He told men to "love your wives, just as Christ loved the church and gave himself up for her" (Ephesians 5:25 NIV). Much of this is a mystery we will be trying to understand and live out all our days. One thing is certain: we are to give ourselves up. Just as Jesus did for his church. Dying to save her. Dying to rescue her. Dying to present her pure to her God. That, gentleman, is the calling of a man.

Isn't it interesting that the stereotype of a modern man is exactly opposite this? You've seen this stereotype played out on the screen. The man is all about himself. His food, his hobbies, his addictions, his deformities, and his vanities dominate his life and the lives in his family. He is one big black hole of self, a giant suck hole of self-interest.

This is too often true of men; but it isn't what they are called to be. Let me tell you a story that will move you with how a man lived out sacrifice. It will astonish you and may change how you live.

Let me introduce you to a hero you have probably never heard of. I think he may be one of the greatest men who ever lived.

His name was Witold (Vee-told) Pilecki. He was born on May 13, 1901, in Russia. These words would have made him wince. His family had been forcibly removed to Russia from their beloved Poland as punishment for a Polish uprising in the 1860s. There were no Polish patriots more passionate than the Pilecki family.

Witold exemplified the Polish soul. He played guitar, painted, wrote poetry, composed songs, gave himself fully to his Catholic faith, and dreamed of a free Polish homeland. He was also fiercely courageous. While still a teenager, he secretly joined a Polish equivalent of the Boy Scouts, though it had been outlawed by Soviet Russia. He fought in guerrilla units during the Soviet-Polish war that followed the First World War and took his examinations to graduate from high school only after that conflict ended. He attended college and then officer training classes, which allowed him to be commissioned as a lieutenant in the Polish army in 1926.

Life moved quickly for him thereafter. He married, had two children, inherited his family's small estate in Belarus, and helped

develop paramilitary units in his home region. He was so effective he was awarded the Silver Cross of Merit in 1938. World War II began the next year.

The invading Germans defeated his 19th Infantry Division on the sixth of September. He fought on with various guerrilla units long after the Polish government had given the country up and taken exile in Paris. Witold stayed in his homeland and helped organize an underground resistance movement—the Tajna Armia Polska, or TAP—the Polish Secret Army. The TAP was built on Christian principles, had no political party affiliation, and grew to as many as twelve thousand men.

Not long after, intelligence reached the TAP that people were being gassed at a prison camp in Auschwitz. Assuming the Allies would liberate the prison camp immediately, Witold and his colleagues began making plans to help. To their dismay, they soon realized the Allies had no such plans. In fact, the TAP wasn't sure the Allies even knew of the camp's existence.

The TAP began preparing to liberate Auschwitz themselves. This is when Witold inscribed his name in the world's Hall of Heroes.

On September 19, 1940, Witold Pilecki tucked forged identity papers into his jacket, kissed his wife and two children good-bye, and intentionally walked into a Nazi roadblock. He was on a mission— a mission to get himself sent to Auschwitz. Once imprisoned, he intended to get intelligence out of the camp to the Polish resistance movement, organize an internal uprising, and boost the morale of Polish inmates.

I want to say it again. Witold Pilecki voluntarily got himself arrested and sent to Auschwitz, the worst of the Nazi extermination camps.

The sketchy journals he was able to smuggle out give some indication of the horrors he endured. They are filled with Nazi butchery, tales of crematoriums, pseudo-medical experiments, and the Nazi delight in killing Poles.

Witold was imprisoned in Auschwitz for 947 days—more than two and a half years—days filled with starvation, beatings, and torture. Yet they were also days of success, for he fulfilled every assignment the Polish Underground gave him. Then he escaped. Had he sat out the rest of the war, no one would have thought less of him. Instead, he joined a British unit and continued to fight Nazis. He was captured in an uprising near Warsaw and held in a prisoner of war camp until the end of the war.

While much of the world celebrated the close of World War II, patriotic Poles quickly realized they had fought Nazi oppression only to end up under equally evil Soviet rule. Witold, ever the patriot, threw himself into this new fight. He again joined an underground movement, taking dangerous assignments to gather intelligence on Soviet operations. He was eventually captured by communist Poles who were in league with the Soviet Union. He was interrogated endlessly, tortured to the threshold of death, and finally found guilty in a farce of a trial in which he received three death sentences.

Just before his execution, he wrote a poem that includes the line, "For though I should lose my life, I prefer it so, than to live, and bear a wound in my heart." This "wound" was knowledge that anyone else should suffer for his spying. He was executed on May 25, 1948, at Warsaw's Mokotow Prison. The details of Pilecki's bravery could not truly emerge until after the collapse of Communism in 1989. He posthumously received the Order of Polonia Restituta in 1995 and the Order of the White Eagle, the highest Polish decoration, in 2006.

His legacy is captured in the words he often gave as his personal credo: *Bóg, Honor, Ojczyzna*—"God, Honor, Country."

He had lived his life for his people and had given everything again and again. He is one of the greatest heroes of Poland, but he is also one of the greatest examples of self-sacrifice we can know. To choose Auschwitz with all its hellish tortures and death required an almost complete surrender of personal preference, inwardly cutting ties with everything dear in this life. This is the essence of being both a man and a patriot. Witold Pilecki is an enduring symbol of both.

We will likely never be asked to have ourselves imprisoned. Most of us will never join a guerrilla movement during a war. We may never be asked to risk our lives.

Simply through the mandate of being men, though, we are asked to surrender our rights and comforts for a higher cause—the responsibility for all we are given as men. Our rights come after the requirements of God, of course, but they also come after whatever is required to serve our wives, to invest in the lives of our children, to stand for righteousness in our communities, or to tend anything else that is within the field assigned to us.

Being a man is a privilege, not an entitlement. It is a surrender of our priority. It is a laying down of our lives, not physically but inwardly—our preferences, our pleasures, sometimes even our dreams. Our version of Witold Pilecki's medals comes in the lives we offer to God, lives we have bled and sweated and prayed and given ourselves for.

This is what it means to be a man.

WHAT THEN WILL YOU DO?
HOW WILL YOU SHOW YOURSELF A MAN?

1. Make sure you are clear on what giving yourself up or laying down your life means. Discuss this with friends, ponder the Scriptures on this point, and think of examples you have known.

2. When has someone surrendered privilege or preference for you in a life-altering way? What did this require? What empowered him or her to do it?

3. Take inventory of your life and the lives in the field assigned to you. Evaluate how you have and how you ought to lay down your life for them. What would this mean? Who are good examples for you? What should this produce in the lives you are responsible for?

4. Drill more deeply into the example of Jesus and his surrender of his life, not just through his death but also in his surrender of privilege and rank. What examples are there for you in this? How can this example empower you to the sacrifices you are called to make?

> ## "A RACE, LIKE AN INDIVIDUAL, LIFTS ITSELF UP BY LIFTING OTHERS UP."
> —*Booker T. Washington, from his "Open Letter" to the Louisiana Constitutional Convention, 1898*

THE THOUSANDTH MAN

One man in a thousand, Solomon says,
Will stick more close than a brother.
And it's worthwhile seeking him half your days
If you find him before the other.
Nine hundred and ninety-nine depend
On what the world sees in you,
But the Thousandth Man will stand your friend
With the whole round world again you.

'Tis neither promise nor prayer nor show
Will settle the finding for 'ee.
Nine hundred and ninety-nine of 'em go
By your looks, or your acts, or your glory.
But if he finds you and you find him.
The rest of the world don't matter;
For the Thousandth Man will sink or swim
With you in any water.

You can use his purse with no more talk
Than he uses yours for his spendings,
And laugh and meet in your daily walk
As though there had been no lendings.
Nine hundred and ninety-nine of 'em call
For silver and gold in their dealings;
But the Thousandth Man he's worth 'em all,
Because you can show him your feelings.

His wrong's your wrong, and his right's your right,
In season or out of season.
Stand up and back it in all men's sight—
With that for your only reason!
Nine hundred and ninety-nine can't bide
The shame or mocking or laughter,
But the Thousandth Man will stand by your side
To the gallows-foot—and after!

—RUDYARD KIPLING

PRESENCE

THERE IS A FEATURE OF MANHOOD I HAVE OBSERVED WITH total fascination over the years. You rarely hear about it because it is so difficult to describe and not particularly easy to live. Still, it is one of the great powers a man has for doing the good he is called to do.

Remember that one of the Manly Maxims we are digesting in these pages is "Manly men tend their fields." The aspect of manhood I'm about to explain here grows from this Manly Maxim, the second of our four pillars. I have learned that when a man is a genuine man and tends his field with devotion and to the glory of God, he receives both authority and grace for that field. He has weight in that field, occupies it for the good of others. He stands within it and somehow permeates it at the same time. He has rank. His spirit covers it.

I like to say it this way: *true men radiate.*

I mean nothing occult or from the pages of science fiction in saying this. I simply mean that part of the grace given to men who tend their fields is they radiate—What is it? Power? Protection? A benevolent force field?—for the good of all they are responsible for.

This is easier to illustrate than it is to describe. In the days when I routinely picked up my children from school, my daughter noticed something and mentioned it to me several times. You should know that my daughter is a real beauty. On the occasions when I would go inside her school rather than wait in the parking lot, I would often see her talking to a boy. This was certainly nothing unusual. Sometimes the boy would have his back toward me, and Elizabeth, who was facing him, could see me over his shoulder.

She has told me that nearly always, when I entered the room and began walking toward her, something about the boy's approach to her would change. It was not that the boy was being inappropriate; she would not have allowed that. It was that the boy became gentler, a bit more respectful, even a bit bashful. Elizabeth knew the young man couldn't see me but she believed he somehow felt my presence.

Now, I'm Elizabeth's father. Everything that concerns her is in me and in my field of responsibility. Of course a boy will feel something different when I'm in the room and he's talking to my daughter, even if he doesn't know I am there. I radiate authority and protection, particularly toward Elizabeth, my only daughter.

I was told of another very powerful illustration of this truth when I was embedded with our American troops in Iraq in 2005. There had been some scandals involving soldiers abusing prisoners in those days, and I spent extensive time with some of the chaplains who had helped correct these situations. The chaplains spoke often of "ministry by presence." For example, they had learned over the years that if a chaplain was present when prisoners were interrogated or disciplined, abuses seldom occurred.

This had nothing to do with the fact that chaplains in the US military are officers. There were officers present when some of the abuses occurred. This wasn't about rank. It was about the moral and spiritual presence the chaplains carried into the room. They changed the unseen environment. Guards commented on this time and again. Usually the chaplains did not say a word, and often the interrogators or handlers of prisoners had not even seen the chaplain when their behavior started changing. There was simply a force for good in the room when chaplains were present. In my informal way of labeling this dynamic, the chaplains radiated.[46]

I think this is a feature of righteous manhood.

The most dramatic example of this radiating I ever witnessed was during the unforgettable day I spent with the legendary UCLA basketball coach John Wooden. It happened completely by accident. I attended a fairly well-known university during my undergraduate days and on a spring morning in 1978 I was awakened by a call from the school's vice president of public relations telling me that John Wooden wanted to tour the campus. Would I accompany him?

Perhaps you can imagine how eagerly I shouted, "Yes!"

I had followed Coach Wooden's career enthusiastically, had read his wonderful book *They Call Me Coach*, and had tried to live out his philosophy. I mean, there wasn't a day that went by that I didn't think of one of his maxims or motivate myself by remembering one of his stories. To spend some hours with this builder of young men felt like a gift from heaven.

I remember almost everything about that day. He was with his sweet wife, Nell, and they must have sensed that I was a homesick college student. They took me under their wing for about six hours, and it changed me in ways I am still discovering.

I couldn't believe my good fortune. There I was, riding around in one of the school's golf carts with *the* John Wooden and his wife while they asked questions of me and gave me advice. Coach even spoke with me about Bill Walton and Kareem Abdul Jabar as if we were all buddies. I was nineteen and probably never stopped yammering once Coach allowed me into his world, but he was nothing but gracious.

I'll tell my grandchildren about that day, but what I will be most eager for them to understand is the power of John Wooden's presence. He was a man committed to God. He had worked hard to overcome his background and his failures, and in time he had led many fierce competitors in epic athletic contests. You felt it. All of it. It radiated from him. There was a steely authority wrapped in a grandfather's tenderness, and you didn't know whether to hug him or come to attention.

It wasn't just me who felt this, either, starstruck teenager that I was. I remember that we walked into the school's athletic facility and stood way off the center court to watch basketball practice. It was not five minutes before one of the lead players started walking our way. We weren't standing in the direction of a locker room or anything that player needed. He was pulled. In later years when I saw the movie *Field of Dreams*, I knew what one character meant when he said, "People won't even know why they are coming. But they will."

I know it sounds odd, but this player started toward us with no purpose at all and in the middle of a practice. He was completely shocked to see the greatest basketball coach in the world standing just off the court.

This happened over and over again. Coach would enter a room— say, the school's main student cafeteria—and he would pull to the side, out of the way. I would see people with their backs to us straighten in their chairs and start looking around for the source of what they felt. I had never seen anything like it at the time. I've seen it many times since, now that I know what it is.

What I was feeling, what nearly everyone nearby was feeling, was the emanation of the life Coach had lived. It was as though the good and noble of all his life experience and of all his powers of command distilled into the spirit that radiated from him.

If the dynamic I'm describing is even close to reality, it is no wonder people felt such a powerful force flowing from this man. He had come into the world in the Indiana of 1910. Among a people devoted to basketball, young Wooden led his high school team to the state championship finals three years in a row. He attended Purdue University, where he was a star player, the first to be named a three-time consensus All-American. He played professionally after college before the navy called and he spent three years as a young officer during World War II.

When he returned to Indiana, he coached basketball at Indiana State, accumulating championships and crafting a philosophy of achievement that began to remake the lives of many of his players. Finally, in 1948, he became the head coach at the University of California, Los Angeles. From that year until his retirement in 1975—a twenty-seven-year career—John Wooden won ten national championships. He was awarded every honor possible for a college basketball coach. There has been no one like him since. In the nine years after John Wooden retired, four men tried to fill his shoes. All failed. Many called him the greatest coach in history. He died on June 4, 2010, four months and ten days shy of his one-hundredth birthday. His was a life well lived.

No wonder you felt the man's spirit before you saw him. No wonder a day in his presence changed your life. I wasn't alone in what I experienced, though. My favorite story about him is one he often told himself with a laugh. It seems a star player had gone on from UCLA and Coach Wooden's tutelage to play professionally. This man had done well and become both rich and famous. He appreciated Coach's influence and said so often, but he had also begun to see himself as an equal.

This famous pro returned to UCLA after some years and spent time with his old mentor. When the player arrived, he announced to Coach that he felt it was more appropriate for him to call Coach by his first name. After all, this player had become a man of status. So for the first hours of this visit, it was, "John this," and "John that." The player just wore out Coach's first name in order to assert his own sense of importance.

Coach was gracious and interested, as he nearly always was with his players—and nineteen-year-old tour guides. But it all became too much for the visiting player. He finally broke down and blurted out, "I can't do it. I just can't!"

"Can't do what?" Wooden asked.

"I just can't call you by your first name. It just isn't right! You are Coach. You always will be. Trying to call you John is just pride. I'm sorry."

Later, this player said, "You just feel this force coming from the man and the last thing it makes you want to do is be all chummy with him. You want to do what he tells you to do. You want to please him. You might even want to fall down and worship. What you don't want to do is call him John."

In my own small teenage way, I knew what this wealthy pro basketball player was saying. John Wooden radiated something powerful, something that arose from his life, something that surrounded you, something that drew you in and made you better. To be with him was to be in his world, even if you were actually standing in your own world. He was a great man, a great spirit, and you felt it every moment you were in his presence.

Gentlemen, I tell you this story not to brag about my moments with a man who probably did not remember my name forty-eight hours later. I tell you because I believe that all these examples, Coach Wooden's in particular, set a benchmark for righteous manhood.

Now, let's not be idiots. Don't sit at dinner with your family tomorrow night and try to push out some invisible force like a four-year-old straining to do his business on the toilet. No, if your version of manhood is principled and holy and turned toward the good of others, it will simply radiate—as it should.

Some might ask why, if this is true, do I even bother to mention it? It is because while I'm urging you to consider that true manhood is action, I also want you to recognize that once you begin acting like a man, you will have the presence that comes with being a man—and that presence is more important, more impactful, than much petty doing.

When you are a dutiful, righteous man standing in your field and forbidding evil by your very presence, your son does not smart off to your wife. Something in the boy, and in the invisible world that might try to influence him, knows you will descend like a jaguar from a tree to protect your wife and ensure discipline—not in violence but as a righteous force. And something in your son knows that he's under the same force field of protection too.

No one mistreats your wife when you are there. She's your queen. You've spent years loving, tending, serving, and guiding her. To all that would harm her, here's the message: *No.* That's it. Just . . . *No. I'm here. She's mine. I'm hers. I've prayed and fasted and stood by her. There isn't any insecurity in me about this. Just calm righteous certainty. Don't mess with her. I'm standing right here—and the God who loves her is with me. Back off.*

And that's how it works. In your home. In your marriage. In your parenting. In your church and your community. Men stand. Men radiate. Men carry something holy and strong for the good of all they've been assigned. It isn't automatic. It comes from doing manhood over time, in the same way John Wooden radiated the essence of what he had become over time.

But it comes. And, my God, it's a beautiful thing.

WHAT THEN WILL YOU DO?
HOW WILL YOU SHOW YOURSELF A MAN?

1. True masculine authority does not come from having a penis or a position. It comes from prayer. It comes from a history of investing. It comes from manning the ramparts of your field. How do you stack up against this definition? Get with some friends and explore these matters carefully in one another's lives. Then, you know what to do. Get busy. Repent. Rebuild. Reengage. Repair. And, in the appropriate ways, reassert.

2. Without saying much to anyone outside the band of brothers I've mentioned, walk the invisible walls of your field, your home and family first. Are there holes? Is someone tormented? In decline? Under attack? Swept away by some unclean force? You know what I'm asking. Then again, you know what to do. Patch the walls in prayer first, then in whatever is required of a loving, gentle, secure, powerful man.

3. Keep this in mind. Being replaces excessive doing. You know how important doing is, if for no other reason than what has been said in these pages. But in the same way you can mess up a golf swing by overswinging, and you can damage your car by overservicing, you can overdo in manly duties. Being replaces excessive doing. Not normal doing. Excessive doing. But first, act wisely. Don't try to compensate for insecurity by doing. It won't work, and it won't bear righteous fruit.

"WE CONVINCE BY OUR PRESENCE."

—*Walt Whitman, from "Song of the Open Road,"* Leaves of Grass *(1900)*

EPILOGUE: THE STORY OF TAYLOR

GENTLEMEN, I WANT TO CLOSE THIS BOOK BY TELLING YOU one more story. I hope it will make you want to act, and act in very much the same way the men in this story did.

There is a church I know and love very much. Its members are nearly all African American, and what is most remarkable about this church is its amazing ministry to men. Frankly, it's the best I've ever seen—bold, fiery, effective, and fun, measured by how men live loving and righteous lives in their homes and their communities. It is wonderful.

The main reason it's wonderful is a man we'll call Taylor. He had the ability to rally men to the example of Jesus and to fulfilling their destinies in this world. He also had an infectious laugh, gave a bone-crushing hug, and could out-eat anyone in the state.

Taylor's ministry to men rocked on for years, changing lives and impacting the community. Well, the thing happened that often happens in churches. A new pastor. A shift in priorities. A new budget. By the time it had all settled, Taylor got hurt and left the church. And he really left the church. He wouldn't talk to anybody. He completely cut himself off. Taylor's wife told some of the men that he had locked himself in his house and wouldn't come out.

This went on for a number of weeks, and no one did anything. Everyone seemed to think Taylor would eventually "get over his mad" and get back to his life. But he didn't, and more weeks went by.

Finally, two of the men in the ministry were talking and one of them said, "You know, I don't want to turn to you in five years and say, 'I wonder what happened to old Taylor. He sure was a good guy. I wonder how he's doing.' We had some pretty special times together, and I'm just not going to sit by and let him drift away. I'm just not going to do it!"

Both men agreed and decided to start talking to all the other men. Then together these men came up with the most astounding plan I've ever seen come out of a church men's ministry.

Within forty-eight hours, these guys had set up camp in Taylor's yard. About 150 of them. They had decided Taylor was going to come out if they had to stay there—on a rotating schedule so men could work their jobs—for the rest of the year if they had to, but they weren't going to let Taylor go.

Picture it: more than 150 African American men camping in Taylor's big old yard with electric lines running from neighboring houses to power the televisions and the refrigerators. About twenty grills and smokers are working up some of the best barbecue in the world. These are men, after all. They don't plan to starve! And there are great big signs all over the place: "Taylor. Come Out. We Love you!" "Taylor, You're an Idiot. Get Out Here!" "Taylor, We Know Where You Live!"

One of the leaders told me later, "We had some fun, but don't think this wasn't a sacrifice. Black men don't camp. But we decided we would do it for Taylor."

This went on for days. Taylor never came out. But our men had come to settle in for the long haul.

All of this must have ticked Taylor off, because on the third day the police came. Taylor had called them. When Taylor's wife and some of the leaders explained what was going on, one of the policemen said, "I wish the guys in our church loved each other this way. Don't worry. We've got this." Then the two cops just drove off. No one knew what they meant by, "We've got this."

The next day, the police came back. They walked through the crowd of men without saying a word and rang the front doorbell. No one answered. One of the officers shouted, "Sir, are you in there? Sir, are you okay? We've had a call that you might not be safe. Sir, you'll need to come to the door to let us know you're okay. Sir, are there guns in there?"

Of course, no one had called the police. These officers had decided to help.

Finally, Taylor came to the door, and the men camping in his yard exploded with cheers, which lasted until Taylor finished his chat with the officers and went back inside.

But the police came back. Twice a day. And not the same policemen, either. Different guys. Apparently the first two had let the entire police department in on what was happening, and they all agreed to help. So twice a day a patrol car pulled up to Taylor's house. Twice a day policemen rang the doorbell. Twice a day one of them shouted that they had received a call and needed to make sure Taylor was all right. And twice a day, the men in that yard got to scream their love for Taylor.

On the sixth day, someone looked up on the porch and there was Taylor—crying his eyes out and sputtering how sorry he was.

And Taylor came out.

This is a true story. In fact, I'm not telling you where this happened because I'm not completely sure that what the policemen did wasn't some violation of regulations.

I've told this story, though, because it is almost a picture of wounded manhood in our age. And what's the answer? Men need to bring men in. Men need to stand for other men. Men need to rescue the men who are adrift. Men need the presence of other valiant men—both living and dead—to draw them out to what they are meant to be.

That's it. That's the story. And at the heart of it is the simple truth we started with. Don't sit around talking so that years from now you're wondering what happened to your life. Act. Act now. Act like a man. Do what men do. There's time for change, and God is with you.

What then will you do? How will you show yourself a man?

WANTED: A MAN TO LEAD

There isn't a boy but wants to grow
Manly and true at heart,
And every lad would like to know
The secrets we can impart.
He doesn't want to slack or shirk—
Oh, haven't you heard him plead?
He'll follow a man at play or work
If only the man will lead.

Where are the men to lead today,
Sparing an hour or two?
Teaching the boy the game to play
Just as a man should do?
Village & slums are calling—"Come,
Here are the boys!" Indeed,
Who can tell what they might become
If only the man would lead.

Where are the men to lend a hand?
Echo it far & wide—
Men who will rise in every land,
Bridging the "Great Divide."
Nation & flag & tongue unite
Joining each class & creed.
Here are the boys who would do right—
But where are the men to lead?

—AUTHOR UNKNOWN

PART THREE

How many a man has dated a new era in
his life from the reading of a book.

—*Henry David Thoreau, from* Walden;
or, Life in the Woods *(1854)*

Movies are the literature of our time.

—*Stephen Mansfield, from a speech
delivered at Belmont University, 2007*

Let men be wise by instinct if they can, but
when this fails be wise by good advice.

—*Sophocles, from his play* Antigone

When power leads man toward arrogance, poetry
reminds him of his limitations. When power
narrows the area of man's concern, poetry reminds
him of the richness and diversity of existence.
When power corrupts, poetry cleanses.

—*John F. Kennedy, remarks upon receiving an
honorary degree, Amherst College, October 26, 1963*

FIFTY QUOTES FOR MANLY MEN

"Every moment and every event
of every man's life on earth plants
something in his soul."

—Thomas Merton, from New Seeds of Contemplation *(1961)*

"I learned that courage was not the absence
of fear, but the triumph over it. . . . The
brave man is not he who does not feel
afraid, but he who conquers that fear."

—Nelson Mandela, from Long Walk to Freedom *(1995)*

"Every man must decide whether he will walk in the light of creative altruism or in the darkness of destructive selfishness."

—*Martin Luther King Jr., recorded in* The Words of Martin Luther King, Jr., *by Coretta Scott King (1983)*

"The ultimate measure of a man is not where he stands in moments of comfort and convenience, but where he stands at times of challenge and controversy."

—*Martin Luther King Jr., from* Strength to Love *(1963)*

"We live in a feminist and effeminate culture. Because of this, at best, as a people we are uneasy with masculinity, and with increasing regularity, whenever it manages to appear somehow, we call for someone to do something about it."

—*Douglas Wilson, from* Future Men *(2001)*

"The central problem of every society is to define appropriate roles for the men."

—*Margaret Mead, from* Male and Female: A Study of the Sexes in a Changing World *(1968)*

"You can fake virtue for an audience.
You can't fake it in your own eyes."

—Ayn Rand, from The Fountainhead *(1943)*

"Happiness does not consist in amusement.
In fact, it would be strange if our end were
amusement, and if we were to labor and
suffer hardships all our life long merely
to amuse ourselves. . . . The happy life
is regarded as a life in conformity with
virtue. It is a life which involves effort
and is not spent in amusement."

—Aristotle, from The Nicomachean Ethics

"These virtues are formed in man by
his doing the actions . . . The good of
man is a working of the soul in the way
of excellence in a complete life."

—Aristotle, from The Nicomachean Ethics

"What virtue is there in a man who
demonstrates goodness because he has
been bred to it? It is his habit from youth.
But a man who has known unkindness and
want, for him to be kind and charitable
to those who have been the cause of his
misfortunes, that is a virtuous man."

—Deanna Raybourn, from Silent on the Moor *(2009)*

"The difference between the old and the new education will be an important one. Where the old initiated, the new merely 'conditions.' The old dealt with its pupils as grown birds deal with young birds when they teach them to fly; the new deals with them more as the poultry-keeper deals with young birds—making them thus or thus for purposes of which the birds know nothing. In a word, the old was a kind of propagation—men transmitting manhood to men; the new is merely propaganda."

—*C. S. Lewis, from* The Abolition of Man *(1943)*

"Virtue is a state of war, and to live in it we have always to combat with ourselves."

—*Jean-Jacques Rousseau, from* Julie, or the New Heloise, *trans. from* Julie, ou la nouvelle Héloïse *(1761)*

"There is nothing so baleful to the small man as the shade of a great one."

—*Washington Irving, from "The Author's Account of Himself," first installment of* The Sketch Book of Geoffrey Crayon, Gent. *(1819–1820)*

"What the superior man seeks is in himself. What the small man seeks is in others."

—*Confucius, from* The Ethics of Confucius, *Analects, bk. xv (1915)*

"How many a man has dated a new era in his life from the reading of a book."

—*Henry David Thoreau, from* Walden;
or, Life in the Woods *(1854)*

"You can discover what your enemy fears most by observing the means he uses to frighten you."

—*Eric Hoffer, from* The Passionate State of Mind *(1955)*

"Worry is rushing into the future and viewing it apart from the grace of God."

—*Rice Brocks, on Twitter, 2012*

"The small man gossips. The average man lets him. The great man stays silent and allows what is said of him to make him greater still."

—*Stephen Mansfield*

"Society everywhere is in conspiracy against the manhood of every one of its members. The virtue most requested is conformity. Self-reliance is its aversion. It loves not realities and creators, but names and customs."

—*Ralph Waldo Emerson, "Self-Reliance"*
(essay), from Essays: First Series *(1841)*

"Adversity toughens manhood, and the
characteristic of the good or the great man
is not that he has been exempt from the evils
of life, but that he has surmounted them."

—*Patrick Henry, from "The Southern Literary
Messenger," quoted in* Patrick Henry: Life,
Correspondence, and Speeches *(1891)*

"Fathers are to sons what blacksmiths are
to swords. It is the job of the blacksmith not
only to make a sword but also to maintain
its edge of sharpness. It is the job of the
father to keep his son sharp and save him
from the dullness of foolishness. He gives
his son that sharp edge through discipline."

—*Steve Farrar, from* King Me: What Every Son
Wants and Needs from His Father *(2006)*

"That's what fathering is all about. It's
mentoring and equipping your son to
become a man who will assume the
family leadership for the next generation.
You have no higher calling in life. It
is your God-given assignment."

—*Steve Farrar,* King Me

"Be the man you wish your father was,
and you don't have to keep saying,
'But my father wasn't around.'"

—*Anonymous*

"If a man hasn't discovered something
he will die for, he isn't fit to live."

—*Martin Luther King Jr., from his speech in
Detroit, Michigan (June 23, 1963)*

"Men, in a word, must necessarily be
controlled either by a power within them
or by a power without them; either by the
Word of God or by the strong arm of man;
either by the Bible or by the bayonet."

—*Robert Winthrop, from a speech to the Massachusetts
Bible Society, quoted in* Robert Winthrop, Addresses
and Speeches on Various Occasions *(1852)*

"That which thy fathers bequeathed thee;
Earn it anew if thou would'st possess it."

—*Ancient Celtic maxim*

"The things a man has to have are hope and confidence in himself against odds, and sometimes he needs somebody, his pal or his mother or his wife or God, to give him that confidence. He's got to have some inner standards worth fighting for or there won't be any way to bring him into conflict. And he must be ready to choose death before dishonor without making too much song and dance about it. That's all there is to it."

—*Clark Gable, quoted in* The Honeycomb
by Adela Rogers St. Johns (1969)

"How beautiful maleness is, if it finds its right expression."

—*D. H. Lawrence, from* Sea and Sardinia *(1921)*

"Because there is very little honor left in American life, there is a certain built-in tendency to destroy masculinity in American men."

—*Norman Mailer, from* Cannibals and Christians,
"Petty Notes on Some Sex in America" (1966;
first published in Playboy 1962–1963)

"It is not the critic that counts; not the man who points out how the strong man stumbles or the doer of deeds could have done them better. The credit belongs to the man who is actually in the Arena, whose face is marred by dust and sweat and blood; who strives valiantly; who errs and comes short again and again, because there is no effort without error and shortcoming; but he who does actually strive to do the deed; who knows the great devotion; who spends himself in a worthy cause, who at the best, knows in the end the triumph of high achievement, and who at the worst, if he fails while daring greatly, knows that his place shall never be with those cold and timid souls, who know neither victory nor defeat."

—*Theodore Roosevelt, from his "Citizenship in a Republic"*
speech on April 23, 1910, at the Sorbonne, Paris, France

"All men dream, but not equally. Those who dream by night in the dusty recesses of their minds wake in the day to find that all was vanity; but the dreamers of the day are dangerous men, for they may act their dream with open eyes, and make it possible."

—*T. E. Lawrence, from* Seven Pillars of Wisdom *(1922)*

"I wish to preach, not the doctrine of ignoble ease, but the doctrine of the strenuous life, the life of toil and effort, of labor and strife; to preach that highest form of success which comes, not to the man who desires mere easy peace, but to the man who does not shrink from danger, from hardship, or from bitter toil, and who out of these wins the splendid ultimate triumph."

—*Theodore Roosevelt, from his "The Strenuous Life"*
speech in Chicago, Illinois, on April 10, 1899

"We laugh at honor and are shocked to find traitors in our midst. We castrate and then bid the geldings be fruitful."

—*C. S. Lewis, from* The Abolition of Man *(1943)*

"Years ago manhood was an opportunity for achievement, and now it is a problem to overcome."

—*Garrison Keillor, from* The Book of Guys: Stories *(1994)*

"A man is at his youngest when he thinks he is a man, not yet realizing that his actions must show it."

—*Mary Renault, from* The King Must Die *(1988)*

"This story shall the good man teach his son;
And Crispin Crispian shall ne'er go by,
From this day to the ending of the world,
But we in it shall be remember'd;
We few, we happy few, we band of brothers;
For he to-day that sheds his blood with me
Shall be my brother; be he ne'er so vile,
This day shall gentle his condition:
And gentlemen in England now a-bed
Shall think themselves accursed
they were not here,
And hold their manhoods
cheap whiles any speaks
That fought with us upon Saint Crispin's day."

—*William Shakespeare, from* Henry V, *act 4, scene 3*

"In this life-long fight, to be waged by every
one of us singlehanded against a host of foes,
the last requisite for a good fight, the last proof
and test of our courage and manfulness, must
be loyalty to truth—the most rare and difficult
of all human qualities. For such loyalty, as
it grows in perfection, asks ever more and
more of us, and sets before us a standard of
manliness always rising higher and higher."

—*Thomas Hughes, from* The Manliness of Christ *(1880)*

"I long to have the children feel that there is nothing in this world more attractive, more earnestly to be desired than manhood in Jesus Christ."

—*Henry Ward Beecher, reported by Josiah Hotchkiss Gilbert in* Dictionary of Burning Words of Brilliant Writers *(1895)*

"The man, whom I call deserving the name, is one whose thoughts and exertions are for others rather than himself."

—*Walter Scott, quoted by Charles D. Cleveland in* English Literature of the Nineteenth Century *(1857)*

"Man seeks, in his manhood, not orders, not laws and peremptory dogmas, but counsel from one who is earnest in goodness and faithful in friendship, making man free."

—*Dietrich Bonhoeffer, from "The Friend" (1952)*

"It is very sad for a man to make himself servant to a single thing; his manhood all taken out of him by the hydraulic pressure of excessive business."

—*Theodore Parker, quoted by Tryon Edwards in* A Dictionary of Thoughts: Being a Cyclopedia of Laconic Quotations from the Best Authors, Both Ancient and Modern *(1891)*

"This is the test of your manhood: How much is there left in you after you have lost everything outside of yourself?"

—*Orison Swett Marden, from "After Failure,—What?"*
published in Success Magazine, *January 1905*

"Some men feel their masculinity can only be proven if they play out in their own life all the locker-room stories, smugly confident that what a wife doesn't know won't hurt her. The truth is, somehow, way down inside, without her ever finding lipstick on the collar or catching a man in the flimsy excuse of where he was till three AM, a wife does know, and with that knowing, some of the magic of this relationship disappears. There are more men griping about marriage who kicked the whole thing away themselves than there can ever be wives deserving of blame."

—*Ronald Reagan, from a letter to his son, Michael Reagan, June 1971, just before his wedding*

"There is an old law of physics that you can only get out of a thing as much as you put in it. The man who puts into the marriage only half of what he owns will get that out."

—*Ronald Reagan, letter to his son, Michael Reagan*

"Any man can find a twerp here and there who will go along with cheating, and it doesn't take all that much manhood. It does take quite a man to remain attractive and to be loved by a woman who has heard him snore, seen him unshaven, tended him while he was sick and washed his dirty underwear. Do that and keep her still feeling a warm glow and you will know some very beautiful music."

—*Ronald Reagan, letter to his son, Michael Reagan*

"All daring and courage, all iron endurance of misfortune make for a finer and nobler type of manhood."

—*Theodore Roosevelt, from his "Address to*
Naval War College," June 2, 1897

"History is strewn with the wrecks of nations which have gained a little progressiveness at the cost of a great deal of hard manliness and have thus prepared themselves for destruction as soon as the movements of the world gave a chance for it."

—*Walter Bagehot, from "The Use of Conflict,"*
in Physics and Politics *(1872)*

"There is no more contemptible type of human character than that of the nerveless sentimentalist and dreamer who spends his life in a weltering sea of sensibility and emotion, but who never does a manly concrete deed."

—*William James, from* The Principles of Psychology, Volume 1, *originally published in 1890*

"Life is too short to be little. Man is never so manly as when he feels deeply, acts boldly and expresses himself with frankness and with fervor."

—*Benjamin Disraeli, from* Coningsby; *or* The New Generation *(1844)*

"In times past there were rituals of passage that conducted a boy into manhood, where other men passed along the wisdom and responsibilities that needed to be shared. But today we have no rituals. We are not conducted into manhood; we simply find ourselves there."

—*Kent Nerburn, from* Letters to My Son: A Father's Wisdom on Manhood, Life, and Love *(1994)*

THE TEN ESSENTIAL BOOKS
FOR MANLY MEN

Wild at Heart: Discovering the Secret of a Man's Soul, John Eldredge

This book gave Christian men, and perhaps men of faith generally, the tools for understanding and living out the essential passions of manhood. It also gave them permission to take seriously the "wildness" in their souls. This is a very important book. My favorite sentiment is one Eldredge expresses in a variety of ways: "You ask me, 'Where are the men?' I say, 'You have made them women.'"

The Book of Man: Readings on the Path to Manhood, William Bennett

Former secretary of education William Bennett has given men a great gift in this book. It is filled with the reflections, speeches, biographies, and seminal writings of some of the most esteemed men in history. From Shakespeare's rousing St. Crispin's Day speech in *Henry V* to an essay on fencing, from the description of a critical moment in Lincoln's youth to the thoroughly relevant thoughts of Seneca, this magnificent volume allows a man to steep his soul in the thoughts and dreams of our fathers.

Halftime: Moving from Success to Significance, Bob Buford

There is no better book than Buford's on the transition a man must make in midlife in order to fulfill his purpose and finish his life well. Read it in youth to know what is coming. Read it in midlife so you have a plan. Read it in old age to understand what you have done and can lead others in the same path.

Every Man's Battle: Winning the War on Sexual Temptation One Victory at a Time, Steve Arterburn

Arterburn does what righteous fathers and brothers ought to have done for us had they existed in our lives: teach us how to stand down sexual temptation in order to live rich, exciting sex lives as God intended. There isn't a man who should be without this book.

Future Men, Douglas Wilson

Calling young boys "thunder puppies," Wilson teaches parents how to respect the emerging manhood in their sons while providing the safe, consistent discipline that allows manhood to thrive, strong and secure.

The Art of Manliness: Classic Skills and Manners for the Modern Man, Brett and Kate McKay

I love the Art of Manliness empire in all its manifestations. The absolutely essential website. The books. The podcasts. You simply don't want to be without the McKays' help in your pursuit of vital manhood. You will learn how to carve a turkey one day, how to maintain manly friendships the next, and on the third you will be moved by a discussion of the manly virtues in the Middle Ages. Wonderful.

The Compleat Gentlemen: The Modern Man's Guide to Chivalry, Brad Miner

This book is both a history and a fiery call to arms, a framing of manhood in achievable terms and the altar call after the sermon. Men, says Miner, must learn to become warriors, lovers, and monks. He's right.

The Code of Man: Love, Courage, Pride, Family, Country, Walter Newell

In these pages we find a searing analysis of our generation's masculine crisis, a moving assurance of the truth that men still yearn to be men and the compass by which to navigate our way home to transforming manhood.

Raising a Modern Day Knight: A Father's Role in Guiding His Son to Authentic Manhood, Robert Lewis

The title tells us what we need to know of this book. Lewis defines manhood in knightly terms and teaches us to make exceptional, chivalrous men of our sons. My son is an exceptional man, but I wish this book had existed when I began my life as a father.

Healing the Masculine Soul: God's Restoration of Men to Real Manhood, Gordon Dalby

I know, I know. I dismissed approaches of this kind at the beginning of this book, but only from these pages, not from the list of matters of pressing concern to modern men. This is a classic. I know few men who do not need it.

THE TEN ESSENTIAL
MOVIES FOR MANLY MEN

Seabiscuit

In the 1930s, the oddly shaped, undersized racehorse Seabiscuit was the subject of more newspaper column inches than either Adolph Hitler or Franklin Roosevelt. The lessons for manly men arise from the lives of three men who must overcome failure and dysfunction to redeem themselves and win with their magnificent little horse.

Chariots of Fire

In the years just after World War I, two runners compete for glory: one for his God, the other to answer the stinging anti-Semitism of his age with Olympic victory. Lessons of character arise from both these men's lives through the tests of faith and disappointment they face.

The Pursuit of Happy-ness

In this true story, a man falls on hard times but determines to take responsibility for his son and the repositioning of his life. Our hero— played by Will Smith—must endure heartbreak, bigotry, crime, and a spiteful wife during his ascent to a new life and a new legacy for his son. Spoiler alert: the man depicted in the film makes a cameo appearance at the end.

It's a Wonderful Life

This sentimental classic is not only a marvelous period piece, but it also teaches the essential lesson that our dreams sometimes go unfulfilled because a greater dream intervenes. In addition, the film's portrayal of one man's impact upon his community challenges us to live more meaningfully ourselves. A scene depicting the devastation of the Great Depression upon a small town is alone worth the viewing.

Dead Poets Society

This movie is a Transcendentalist morality play, with Walt Whitman's photograph hovering and Henry David Thoreau's stirring phrases woven throughout. The central theme, though, is the power of literature to inspire and the clash of generations that often results. Lessons of life and manhood fall freely from the script. One example: "Sports is an opportunity for us to have other human beings push us to excel." This is the film that wrote the Latin phrase *carpe diem*— "seize the day"—into our cultural lexicon.

Apollo 13

A "successful failure." That's what NASA called the Apollo 13 mission, which was aborted shortly after its launch in 1970 due to massive technical failure en route to the moon. This film is not only a Ron Howard masterpiece starring Tom Hanks, it is also a reminder that sometimes bringing a failed venture to a satisfying conclusion is a victory. Most men will have opportunity to effect "successful failures" in their lives. Many of the skills of accomplishing this feat are depicted in this visually stunning film. One principle that leaps from the screen: "Failure is not an option!"

The King's Speech

The touching, inspiring tale of England's King George VI striving to overcome his stuttering—just as he replaced his brother on the throne and Europe descended into the horrors of World War II—is both a valuable history lesson and a depiction of how much one man's character can mean to the world. The friendship between a king and a commoner is also a fascinating study of manly bonds overcoming the hindrances of class and power.

Men of Honor

How does a black man in post–World War II America achieve his dream of being a Master Diver in the United States Navy? This was the challenge of Master Chief Petty Officer Carl Brashear, whose genuine struggles inspired this film. Starring Robert De Niro and Cuba Gooding Jr., this film is a study of the manly virtues lived in the face of crushing racism and the arduous battle to master one of the world's most dangerous and difficult professions.

Hoosiers

F. Scott Fitzgerald once wrote, "There are no second acts in American lives." He was wrong, and *Hoosiers*, another true story stirringly told, proves it. A coach with a past tries to redeem himself in a small Indiana town where basketball is holy liturgy and heartland values clash with the passions of the court. The depiction of rural Indiana in the 1950s is achingly beautiful. In the end, history is made and love prevails. The manly lessons learned along the way are invaluable.

The Last Samurai

The warrior code is an essential feature of manly culture. This film is a meditation on this truth as exemplified in Shintoism's bushido code. Written and directed by Edward Zwick and starring Tom Cruise, there are few more powerful depictions of a period, of a culture, and of the bonds of men at arms.

ACKNOWLEDGMENTS

IT IS ONE OF THE ODDITIES OF MY LIFE THAT MY MOTHER SET the vision for the manhood I would aspire to all my days. She had grown up in the home of an army officer who was temporarily paralyzed while fighting in Germany during World War II and who then served as an aide to General Douglas MacArthur in the Far East. She later married a newly minted second lieutenant who would eventually fight in Vietnam and serve as an intelligence chief in Berlin during the bitter days of the Cold War. She knew something of what it meant to be a man and she wanted her son to be one. Her most stinging rebuke usually came in the form of a plea: "Will you be a man?" She was a teacher by nature and often worked lessons of manhood into our long hours of conversation. "That's not what a man does," she would say quietly, perhaps after reading in the newspaper about a crime or a family impoverished by drink. If one of my father's fellow officers behaved heroically, my mother would declare simply, reverently, "Well, he's a *man*," as though the word *man* captured all that was grand and valiant in the world.

How very much I wanted to embody her transcendent vision of manhood. I still do.

I left my parents' home and stepped out into the world when true masculinity was already in crisis. That was in the 1970s. Manliness was perceived as little more than a style. It was signaled by a cologne rather than a condition of soul. It took only a few genuine men in my life to convince me that my generation of males were becoming androgynous and calling it liberation. In time, they would find it wasn't liberating anyone.

Nothing confirmed this for me like the day I spent with UCLA coach John Wooden. Confirmation came also from the years I spent studying and writing about Winston Churchill, unquestionably my hero and my model for manly greatness. Through the years, I've had the privilege of knowing men like Lieutenant General William Boykin, of being embedded with US troops in Iraq, of naming among my friends members of Delta Force, and of walking with men who exhibit honor in arenas as varied as the surgical theater and the community center, Monday Night Football and the high school classroom.

I also remember tearfully thinking that the young man without arms and legs who boarded a bus every morning in downtown Nashville to go to work twenty miles away—and did so with joy and a smile for everyone he passed—was probably the greatest man I had ever seen.

I grew to understand a bit about righteous manhood and loved recounting stories of manly greatness with like-hearted friends. No one exulted in this like my friend Jim Laffoon. He would goad me into describing Churchill, Alfred the Great, or perhaps Lincoln and then would exclaim with delight, "My God! Now that was a man, don't you think, Steve? I mean, he was *man!*" We would talk late into the night, telling tales as though trying to keep a flame of masculinity lit for our generation.

This generational hope is what inspired Joel Miller, my publisher at Thomas Nelson, to envision this book and its design. I am grateful. He is a true manly man who lives out righteous manhood in sacrificial ways few ever see. I could not ask for a better partner in the tumultuous business of books.

My daughter, Elizabeth, helped edit this manuscript and it was sweet to have her thoughtful comments as a guide. As we worked together one day, she told me she hoped her future husband would look something like the men described in these pages. Don't worry, baby; I intend to make sure of it!

Numerous friends contributed material as I wrote. My fellow warrior, David Holland, helped with extensive research. His vision of history was invaluable, as it has been on some of my other projects. Crazed Italian Todd Bulgarino, one of the finest fathers I know, also provided material, as did George Grant and, again, Joel Miller. When General Boykin's foreword arrived, it made me eager to be both a better man and a better writer. I'm honored his spirit hovers over these pages.

Finally, all I am I offer to Bev, whose womanly ways keep me ever in hope of becoming the man she deserves.

NOTES

Legacy

1. Randolph S. Churchill, *Winston S. Churchill: Youth, 1874–1900* (Boston: Houghton Mifflin Company, 1966), 43.
2. Martin Gilbert, *Churchill: A Life* (New York: Henry Holt and Company, 1991), 23.
3. Ibid., 19.
4. Churchill, *Youth*, 189.
5. Winston Churchill, *My Early Life: A Roving Commission* (Macmillan Publishing Company, 1930), 62.
6. William Manchester, *The Last Lion: Winston Spencer Churchill, Visions of Glory, 1874–1932* (New York: Little, Brown and Company, 1983), 188.
7. Ibid., 188–189.

Blessing

8. Gene Smith, *Until the Last Trumpet Sounds: The Life of General of the Armies John J. Pershing* (New York: John Wiley & Sons, Inc., 1998), 290.

Quest

9. Dale L. Morgan, *Jedediah Smith and the Opening of the American West* (Lincoln, NE: Bison Books, University of Nebraska Press, 1964).
10. Jon Krakauer, *Into the Wild* (New York: Villard Books, 1996).

Humor

11. Ian Ker, *G. K. Chesterton: A Biography* (Oxford University Press, 2011), xcv.
12. Dale Alquist, *G. K. Chesterton: The Apostle of Common Sense* (Ignatius Press, 2003), 11–12.

13. Ibid.
14. Ibid.
15. This selection of G. K. Chesterton quotes is taken from Dale Alquist's *G. K. Chesterton: The Apostle of Common Sense* (Ignatius Press, 2003) and Ian Ker's *G. K. Chesterton: A Biography* (Oxford University Press, 2011).
16. These stories can be found in Winston Churchill, *The Irrepressible Churchill, 1874–1965*, Kay Halle, ed. (Cleveland: World Pub. Co., 1966), 1.

Self-Education

17. Randolph S. Churchill, *Winston S. Churchill: Youth, 1874–1900* (Boston: Houghton Mifflin Company, 1966), 322.
18. Merle Miller, *Plain Speaking: An Oral Biography of Harry S. Truman* (New York: Harper and Row, 1980), 69.
19. Robert H. Ferrell, *Off the Record: The Private Papers of Harry Truman* (New York: Harper and Row, 1980), 187.
20. Miller, *Plain Speaking*, 21.
21. David McCullough, *Truman* (New York: Simon and Schuster, 1992), 463.
22. Ibid., 986.

Wildness

23. David McCullough, *Mornings on Horseback* (New York: Simon and Schuster, 1981, 2001), 90.
24. Ibid., 112.
25. Ibid.
26. Nathan Miller, *Theodore Roosevelt* (New York: William Morrow, 1992), 155.
27. Ibid.
28. Edmund Morris, *The Rise of Theodore Roosevelt* (New York: Coward, McCann & Geoghegan, 1979), 298.
29. Thomas Russell, ed., *Life and Work of Theodore Roosevelt* (New York: L. H. Walter, 1919), 116.

Forgiveness

30. "The Lebar Brecc Homily on St. Patrick," from Whitley Stokes, *The tripartite life of Patrick: With other documents relating to that saint* (1887).
31. Paragraph 16 of St. Patrick's *Confessio*, from the Royal Irish Academy under a Creative Commons License, www.confessio.ie/# (accessed 10 April 2013). All quotes following here are from the *Confessio*.
32. Frederick Buechner, *Wishful Thinking: A Theological ABC* (New York: Harper and Row, 1973).

Suffering

33. Letter to John Stuart, 20 January 1841, from Roy P. Basler, Marion Dolores Pratt, and Lloyd A. Dunlap, eds., *The Collected Works of Abraham Lincoln* (New Brunswick: Rutgers University Press, 1953), vol. 1, 228.

34. Douglas L. Wilson and Rodney O. Davis, eds., *Herndon's Informants* (Chicago: University of Illinois Press, 1998), 133, 475.

35. Quoted in Richard Lawrence Miller, "Lincoln's Suicide Poem: Has It Been Found?" *For the People* 6, no. 1 (Spring 2004), 6.

36. Joshua Wolf Shenk, *Lincoln's Melancholy: How Depression Challenged a President and Fueled His Greatness* (New York: Houghton Mifflin Company, 2005), 12.

Vision

37. Rudyard Kipling, *Something of Myself* (Cambridge University Press, 1990), 5–6.

38. Ibid.

39. Ibid., 17.

40. Ibid., 25.

41. William James Dawson, *The Making of Manhood* (New York: Thos. Crowell and Son, 1894), 101.

42. Rudyard Kipling, *Life's Handicap: Being Stories of My Own People* (New York: Doubleday, Page & Company, 1916).

Humility

44. Emmett J. Scott and Lyman Beecher Stowe, *Booker T. Washington: Builder of a Civilization* (New York: Doubleday, Page & Company, 1916), xii.

45. William Mountford, *Euthanasy: Or, Happy Talk Towards the End of Life* (Boston: Wm. Crosby and H. P. Nichols, 1848), 264.

Presence

46. For more on this fascinating episode in our nation's history and on the role military chaplains played, see my *The Faith of the American Soldier* (Charisma House, 2005).

ABOUT THE AUTHOR

STEPHEN MANSFIELD IS A *NEW YORK TIMES* BEST-SELLING author of books about history and contemporary culture. His works include *The Faith of George W. Bush, The Search for God and Guinness, Never Give In: the Extraordinary Character of Winston Churchill, The Faith of Barack Obama,* and *Lincoln's Battle with God.* He is a popular speaker who also coaches leaders worldwide. Mansfield lives in Nashville and Washington D.C. with his wife, Beverly, who is an award-winning songwriter and producer. (StephenMansfield.TV)